HAMSTER

FAMILY PET
GUIDE

A PRACTICAL GUIDE
TO CARING FOR YOUR
HAMSTER

DAVID
ALDERTON

Collins

First published in 2002 by
Collins, an imprint of
HarperCollinsPublishers
77-85 Fulham Palace Road
Hammersmith, London W6 8JB

www.harpercollins.co.uk

Collins is a registered trademark of
HarperCollins Publishers Limited

This edition published in 2011

15 14 13 12 11
10 9 8 7 6 5 4 3 2 1

A catalogue record of this book is
available from the British Library.

ISBN 978-0-00-743670-5

This book was created by SP Creative
Design for HarperCollinsPublishers
Editor: Heather Thomas
Design and Production: Rolando Ugolini

Additional photography:
David Alderton: pages 28, 57, 63, 92, 93
Rolando Ugolini: pages 66, 81

Colour reproduction by
Coloursan, Singapore
Printed and bound by
Printing Express Ltd, Hong Kong

Contents

Introduction

Few pets are easier to look after than hamsters, and they appeal to owners of all ages. Even at holiday times, it is usually quite easy to find a friend or neighbour to look after a hamster while you are away, should you not be able to take your pet with you.

Part of the hamster's appeal stems from its cute appearance. A hamster will occupy little space in a home, and you can enjoy the company of your pet irrespective of whether you live in an apartment or a house with a garden. Hamsters make no noise and have no unpleasant odour associated with them provided that their quarters are kept clean. They are lively, inquisitive creatures, who soon become tame and will recognise their owner by scent if not necessarily by sight. Handling a hamster is quite straightforward, and provided that they are not grasped tightly, they generally do not bite.

Their behaviour is quite fascinating to watch, as they scamper and clamber around their quarters or stuff their cheek pouches with food before scurrying back to their house and eating there. The fact that hamsters tend to sleep for most of the day makes them ideal for owners who are out at work or at school during the daytime, and since they generally live solitary lives, there is no need to worry about them being kept on their own and pining for company in your absence.

Although they are not especially long-lived, hamsters are usually very healthy throughout their lives, and need no routine vaccinations or deworming. In fact, they are relatively inexpensive pets to care for, with the only major item of expenditure being their accommodation.

In the past, only the Syrian Hamster shown here was available to pet-seekers, but a number of other members of this group of rodents, whose representatives range through parts of Europe and the Middle East to Asia, are now being kept as well. This, plus the ever-increasing range of colour and coat varieties that exists in the Syrian Hamster, means that the available choice of pet hamsters has grown greatly over recent years, adding still further to the popularity of these lovable rodents.

CHAPTER ONE

Origins of the pet hamster

Hamsters have now become the most popular of all pet rodents kept in the home, appealing to people of all ages. Yet just 60 years ago, they were hardly known outside the scientific world, only being seen occasionally as zoo exhibits. Today, however, there are five different types from which you are likely to be able to choose as pets.

The best-known of these is the Golden or Syrian Hamster. It is still the most commonly-kept member of the group, in spite of the rapid rise in popularity of the Dwarf Russian Hamsters over recent years. The Campbell's and Winter White forms of the Dwarf Russian are very closely related, and are slightly larger in size than Roborovski's, which is not as widely available at present. The Chinese Hamster is also bred in relatively small numbers, not being as prolific as the Syrian, but generally it can still be acquired without too much difficulty.

CHAPTER
ONE

Hamster homelands

■ **Syrian or Golden Hamster** (*Mesocricetus auratus*)
Lives around Mount Aleppo in Syria. Its precise range is
unclear, especially after a population was recorded from Kilis, in
southern-central Turkey on the Syrian border, in 2000.

■ **Winter White Dwarf Hamster** (*Phodopus sungorus sungorus*)
Lives in eastern Kazakhstan and south-west Siberia.

■ **Campbell's Dwarf Hamster** (*Phodopus sungorus campbelli*)
Lives in Russia, Mongolia and some areas of China.

■ **Roborovski's Dwarf Hamster** (*Phodopus roborovskii*)
Lives in Russia, eastern Kazakhstan, west and southern parts of
Mongolia and neighbouring areas of China.

■ **Chinese or Striped Hamster** (*Cricetulus griseus*)
Lives in Northern China and Mongolia.

The Syrian Hamster

The earliest account of the Syrian Hamster and its habits are
contained in a book published during 1797, describing the
natural history of the area around Mount Aleppo in Syria, which
was written by an English physician, Alexander Russell, and his
brother. It was not until 1839, however, that a specimen was
sent to London and officially recognised, being given a scientific
name. This hamster, known as the type specimen because it was
the first example to be described, is still in the collection of the
Natural History Museum in London. It is slightly smaller in size
than today's domesticated Syrian hamsters.

The first live Syrians seen outside their homeland were
brought to Great Britain during 1880 by James Skene, who had
been the Consul General at the British Embassy in Syria. He
returned with a small group of these rodents to his home in

Edinburgh, Scotland. Although he continued to breed them for over 30 years, his hamsters seem to have attracted little interest as potential pets and the colony ultimately died out.

The rise of the Syrian Hamster

The way in which these hamsters finally achieved their widespread international popularity is rather a strange story. During the 1920s, Professor Adler at the Hebrew University in Jerusalem was investigating the parasitic illness known as leishmaniasis, and he started using Chinese Hamsters in his research, only to discover that they did not breed very well. When he learnt that a fellow scientist, Israel Aharoni, was organising an expedition to the area of Mount Aleppo in Syria, he asked his colleague whether he could bring back some Syrian Hamsters, in the hope that they could be persuaded to breed more reliably.

Aharoni set out in 1930 and, with the assistance of the local people, he located a nest containing a female with eleven young, at the bottom of a burrow 2.5 m (8 ft) deep in a cornfield. They were all transferred immediately to a box, but the mother then killed one of her young pups and had to be removed. Another pup escaped but the team were able to return to the Hebrew

Below: *Syrian Hamsters were originally called Golden Hamsters, but now they exist in many other colours, this name is less commonly used.*

CHAPTER ONE

University with the remaining nine young hamsters. Disaster then struck, however, because using their sharp teeth to great effect, the hamsters managed to chew their way out of their wooden container and five disappeared. This left just a single female and three males, but they prospered in their new surroundings and within a year their numbers had grown to about 150 in total.

Professor Adler then took two pairs of Syrian hamsters to England, supposedly hidden in the pockets of his raincoat, and they passed into the care of Professor Hindle at the Wellcome Bureau of Scientific Research, who was also investigating leishmaniasis. Once again, they bred prolifically and several pairs were donated to the Zoological Society of London in 1932. Five years later, the zoo passed some of its surplus stock on to private breeders, and so began the rise of the Syrian as a pet.

The start of hamster farms

It was also at this time that Syrians were first seen in North America. Again, they were kept initially for scientific research before becoming available to pet seekers, who soon fell under their charm. An unemployed highway engineer called Albert Marsh appreciated the huge potential demand for hamsters after winning one as the result of a bet in the 1940s. This led him to establish the Gulf Hamstery in the town of Mobile, Alabama, and he did much to promote the Syrian as a pet in these early days. Unfortunately, his success proved to be his undoing, as others were soon attracted to commercial hamster breeding and, in the face of intense competition, Marsh's trail-blazing business had collapsed by the mid-1950s.

However, it was not just as pets that these hamsters appealed to people. Particularly in

Left: *Hamsters today are being bred in a growing range of varieties.*

Right: *The sable form of the Syrian
is one of the newer colour forms.*

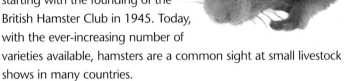

the United Kingdom, keen interest
soon developed in exhibiting them,
and a number of clubs were
established for this purpose,
starting with the founding of the
British Hamster Club in 1945. Today,
with the ever-increasing number of
varieties available, hamsters are a common sight at small livestock
shows in many countries.

The commercial breeding of hamsters began in Britain at a
later stage than in the United States, with enthusiast Percy Parslow
setting up his famous Hamster Farm in 1961. He bred many
thousands each year on these premises at Great Bookham in
Surrey, including a number of the emerging colour varieties. This
trend continues today, with a number of commercial breeders
producing not only Syrians but also both Chinese and Dwarf
Russians to meet the demand from pet seekers.

An amazing thought
Perhaps the most remarkable thing about the rise of the Syrian
Hamster as a pet, however, is the fact that right up until 1971, the
millions of individuals that had been bred in captivity were all
descended from the small family group obtained in that cornfield
over 40 years earlier by Israel Aharoni. Even now, the likelihood is that
any Syrian Hamster that you buy will also have an ancestry tracing
back to those individuals, because very few have since been brought
from the wild into breeding programmes. The main importation was
a group of a dozen individuals that were taken to the United States
from Syria during 1971. There is a record of a single female being
brought to the United Kingdom in 1980, but she never bred.

CHAPTER
ONE

Dwarf Russian Hamsters

The Dwarf Russian Hamsters are a relatively recent introduction by comparison. Campbell's was the first to be seen, with stock having reached the Zoological Society of London in 1963. The numbers of these hamsters increased slowly at first, and it was not until the mid-1970s that Percy Parslow, following the same route as had occurred with the Syrian Hamster, introduced these smaller hamsters to the pet trade.

❖ *Chocolate Banded Campbell's*

The Chinese Hamster

The history of the Chinese Hamster is not as well-documented, but these rodents have certainly been bred in laboratories for longer than their Syrian relative. British records trace the presence of these hamsters back as far as 1919. In the early days, stock is thought to have originated from a number of different locations, including Manchuria in China and Mongolia. However, it appears that the ancestors of those available today are mainly descended from a small group brought back from the vicinity of the capital Beijing (formerly known as Peking) about 1926.

❖ *Dominant Spot Chinese: a mutation*

Winter Whites and Roborovski's

In 1978, the Winter White sub-species of the Dwarf Russian became available from stock that had been held at Queen Mary's College, part of the University of London, since the early 1970s. The Roborovski's has a similar history, being descended from laboratory strains which also became available as pets during this decade. Its small size makes it particularly appealing.

❖ Roborovski's

Above: *This young Roborovski's Hamster is just over two weeks of age. These hamsters are still less commonly seen than their Dwarf Russian relatives.*

CHAPTER TWO

Species and varieties

All of the species of hamster that are now commonly kept as pets have a long history of domestication, extending back over hundreds of generations. In spite of the fact that today's strains were derived from just a very small number of individuals at the outset, they are all remarkably healthy and generally free from any inherited disorders.

S ince hamsters breed so rapidly, when new colours have occurred it has been possible to develop these and establish them quite quickly. Then once the colour variety concerned is considered to be well-established, new judging standards are created for it in show circles. The popularity of some varieties is higher than others, and the more striking and newest colour forms often attract the most attention from breeders. These are also likely to be the most costly, although generally, hamsters are not expensive pets. You may even find that a pet store will be able to obtain a young hamster of a particular colour for you from their suppliers.

CHAPTER TWO

SYRIAN HAMSTERS

As domestication of the Syrian Hamster took place, so an ever-increasing range of colours has been created. Some of these are colour mutations, being the result of an unexpected change in the hamster's genetic make-up, whereas others are colour varieties, which are created by combining various mutations. It is not just changes in coloration that have occurred either, since the texture and length of the fur have also been modified as a result of mutations affecting the hamster's coat.

❖ *Golden Syrian*

Golden Hamsters

The natural colour of the Syrian Hamster is always referred to as Golden, being a rich shade of deep chestnut, showing the

❖ *Dark Golden Syrian*

mahogany ticking on the individual hairs. The underside of the body is predominantly ivory, while the short undercoat, which you can see by parting the hair close to the skin, is greyish. These hamsters also have cheek flashes – darker areas of fur on the face – and well-defined bands called crescents, which match the ivory colour of the fur of the lower abdomen. There is also what is referred to as a chestband, which is golden in colour and extends across this part of the underside of the body. The eyes of the Golden Hamster are black, with the ears being dark grey.

Bear in mind, however, that examples of this form, often described as the Wild-type Agouti, do vary slightly in the depth of colour. Those with paler, fawny golden-brown coloration are described as Light Goldens, whereas in the case of the Dark Golden, the fur is a rich shade of mahogany red, which is broken up with black ticking.

Paler colours

The first of the colour mutations that were recorded in the case of the Syrian Hamster was the Black-eyed Cream, which first appeared during 1951. Since then, both Red-eyed and slightly darker Ruby-eyed Creams have been bred as well. Creams are extremely popular, partly because of their attractive cream colouring, but also because they have acquired a reputation for being very friendly by nature, although there is really no significant difference in temperament between the various colours.

❖ Black-eyed Cream Syrian

For exhibition purposes, look for Cream hamsters that have an even depth of coloration over their coats. It is easy to distinguish the Red-eyed from the Ruby-eyed since it has slightly greyish ears, whereas those of the Ruby-eyed form are pink. As members of the so-called Self group, consisting of a single colour, so these hamsters do not have any contrasting cheek flashes, crescents or chestbands, although their underparts may be slightly paler than the fur elsewhere on their bodies.

❖ Long-haired Red-eyed Cream Syrian

CHAPTER
TWO

White Hamsters

The first White Syrian
Hamster was documented
in 1952 and, today, these
Dark-eared Whites with red
eyes have been joined by
both Black-eyed and Albino
forms. These two more recent
additions to the Self group can be easily

❖ *Dark-eared White Syrian*

distinguished by the colour of their ears, as only Albinos have pink
ears. The white fur in all cases should be of a pure, snow-white
shade, but beware, because it can be easily stained by juicy fresh
foods such as carrots and greenstuff. This can spoil the
appearance of the hamster before a show, and any discoloured
areas of fur will need to be washed carefully beforehand. It is
probably better to withhold such foods just
prior to a show for this reason.

Ivory Hamsters

Slightly darker in colour is the Black-
eyed Ivory, whose fur is a greyish-
cream shade, set against its dark,
almost black ears. There is also a
Red-eyed form of this colour, which
has pinkish-grey ears. In both cases,
as with other Self (single) coloured
hamsters, the coloration of the fur
needs to be even.

Blonde Hamsters

The Blonde is distinguished by its distinctive
creamy-blonde coloration, with a pale grey
undercoat. Its ivory crescent-shaped markings

❖ *Long-haired Albino
Syrian youngster*

correspond to the colour of the belly fur, with the chestband being creamy-blonde. An unusual feature of many Blonde hamsters is that they have a more orange area of fur in the vicinity of the muzzle.

Cinnamon Hamsters

The Cinnamon, another non-self variety, is one of the most colourful forms of the Syrian Hamster. It is a pure shade of rich russet orange, with a slate-blue undercoat and a matching chestband. Ivory crescents and brown cheek flashes are also apparent, while the eyes are red and the ears are brown.

❖ Cinnamon Syrian

There is also a Cinnamon Fawn variety, which is paler, being a pastel shade of orange with light grey underfur. The crescents in this case should be of a very light cream shade, like the belly, while the cheek flashes are pale grey and the eyes are pinkish.

Fawn Hamsters

The Fawn Hamster itself is ruby-eyed, with a coat colour matching its name, and this can be parted to reveal its light slate grey undercoat. The fawn cheek patches provide another means of recognising this variety.

Honey Hamsters

Pale cinnamon orange coloration is also a feature of the coat colour of the Honey, extending over the chestband. The whitish crescents match the colour of the belly, with the cheek flashes being of a cinnamon shade. Pinkish-grey ears and deep red eyes are other characteristic features associated with hamsters of this colour.

▌Shades of grey

Various grey forms of the Syrian hamster
are now quite well established.

Dark and Light Greys

The first grey form to emerge was the
Dark Grey, which was first recorded in
1964, followed by the Light Grey form in
the following year. The Dark form is actually a
pearly-grey shade ticked with black, while slate-
grey coloration is evident at the bases of the
hairs. The cheek flashes are black, offset against ivory
cheek crescents, with the

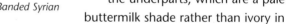

❖ *Light Grey
Syrian*

underparts also being
ivory. The Light Grey is paler
overall, as its name suggests.
It has dark and pale buttermilk
banding running down the
hairs, which become slate-blue
at their bases. If you are in any
doubt as to whether you have
a Light or a Dark Grey, look at
the underparts, which are a pale

❖ *Dark Grey Banded Syrian*

buttermilk shade rather than ivory in
this case, corresponding in colour to the crescents. The chestband is also slate-blue, rather than simply a dark shade of slate.

❖ *Dark Grey
Syrian*

■ Lilac and Champagne Hamsters

The Lilac, too, has a grey tone to its fur, but in this case there is a pinker hue. The eyes are also red rather than black in colour, with the cheek flashes being a warm shade of grey, matching the hamster's undercoat. Both the belly and the crescents are a pale lilac white. A paler grey self form, which is described as Champagne, with a lilac tinge to its coat, has also been bred. This pink-eyed form is self-coloured.

❖ Lilac Syrian

Silver Grey and Smoke Pearl Hamsters

The Silver Grey is another attractive grey form, which has a dark grey undercoat, with a noticeable silvery tone. An even depth of coloration is an important feature of these particular hamsters. Their underparts should be whitish, with the chest band being dark grey. You may also encounter the Smoke Pearl variety on occasions, which is a greyish-cream colour, with a matching chest band. The ears of these hamsters are paler than in the case of the Silver Grey, being a dark shade of grey rather than black.

Beige Hamsters

The Beige is an attractive soft, pale shade of grey, which also has a brownish tone to its fur. The coat is slate-coloured at its base. The belly and crescents are both white in colour, while the cheek flashes themselves are a dark shade of beige, matching the fur on the underside of the chest. The ears correspond in colour to the cheek flashes, with the eyes being black.

Darker variants

The quest to produce a black hamster led to the breeding of what, rather confusingly, was a variety originally known under this name but now called the Sable. This change became necessary thanks to the breeding of the true Black Syrian, which originated in France about 1990, although much of its early development took place in Sweden and it was from here that stock was brought to the United Kingdom.

Black Hamsters

Whereas the Sable was created by the introduction of the dark umbrous gene into Black-eyed Cream bloodlines, the true Black arose as the result of a genuine mutation. The

❖ *Sable Syrian*

Sable does appear black but, on close examination, the base of the coat nearest to the skin is ivory-grey, and this colour usually encircles the eyes. In contrast, the true form of the Black is jet black, although it is not uncommon for these particular hamsters to have small white areas of fur, especially on the feet, but there are no lighter circles of fur around the eyes.

❖ *Chocolate Syrian*

Chocolate, Copper, Rust and Gold Hamsters

Another of the newer, darker colours is the Chocolate, a self form which is dark brown in colour, with matching ears and black eyes. The Copper, too, is a recent addition to the Self group. These particular hamsters can be identified by the coppery colour of their fur, offset against their dark red eyes and greyish ears. The Rust or Guinea

❖ *Rust Piebald Syrian*

Gold also displays a brownish tone in its coat. This suffuses its basically orange fur, with the base colour in this case being a pale slate-grey. The crescents on the face are creamy-ivory, matching the belly fur. The ears are greyish, with a slight brownish-pink tone.

▌Patterned varieties

The first documented mutation to arise in the case of the Syrian was the form known as the Piebald or White Spot, which was first recorded back in 1947. It is so-called because of the white spots or blotches that break up its coloration, with this characteristic having been combined with many of the other colours which have since emerged. Ideally, in good show specimens of this variety, the white and coloured areas should be roughly even in extent, but they can vary greatly. If you choose one of these hamsters, its markings are likely to be quite unique.

❖ *Sable Piebald Syrian*

    In addition to the Piebald, a number of other patterned varieties now exist in the case of the Syrian, although bear in mind that if you are interested in exhibiting hamsters, these are harder to breed with the

required pattern of markings. These are superimposed on the regular coloration, so as a result, in the case of the Banded for example, there should be an area of pure white fur encircling the hamster's body, midway along its back and accounting for a third of its length. The remainder of the fur matches that of the colour variety concerned.

It is possible to create Banded hamsters in all colour varieties therefore, with the exception of white forms. The contrast is most impressive in the case of darker varieties, but often the white banding does not encircle the body consistently. This then spoils the hamster's show potential.

A balance between the coloured and white areas is also an important feature of the Tortoiseshell and White. The patterning in this case should be symmetrical, and the white fur must be clearly defined, not running into the coloured areas, which is a fault known as brindling. The coloured fur in the case of Tortoiseshell and White Hamsters is a yellowish shade, combined

Above: *A litter of young hamsters with a banded patterning. Note the variation in their markings, which will not alter throughout their lives.*

with another colour, often black or, less commonly, chocolate-brown. Mosaic is the description given to a particular type of tortoiseshell patterning where there are spots rather than blotches of colour extending over the body. These, again, must be clearly defined, with the cream coloration also being of an even shade over the body.

Mixing of the coat colours and white hairs is a feature of the White-bellied mutation, however, where the presence of white hairs through the coat causes the body coloration to appear paler than normal. In the case of Roan Syrian Hamsters, there is black ticking alternating with white bands down the individual hairs. This is a case where the ears may be variable in colour, sometimes being dark grey broken with flesh-coloured patches.

Coat variants

Long-haired and Angora hamsters
The most popular coat variant associated with the Syrian is the Long-haired or Angora form, better known in North America as the Teddy, thanks to its cuddly appearance. It was first bred during the early 1970s in the United States and, initially, the desirable long coat was seen at its most impressive in male hamsters, being decidedly less evident in females, although this difference is no longer really apparent in exhibition stock today. Even so, males still usually display a more prominent mane of longer hair around the neck. The overall quality of the coat is

Above: *An adult long-haired Syrian. The hair length is quite variable, depending partly on the hamster's age.*

very important, and it must display good density, rather than being thin and straggly. The hair itself should fall evenly down the sides of the hamster's body.

Self-coloured forms of the Angora are generally most striking, especially as the longer coat removes the clear definition of marked varieties. In some cases, including the Golden itself, both the crescents and cheek flashes are lost, so the hamster looks less colourful than its short-coated counterpart.

In many commercially-bred hamsters of this type, however, the hair is not consistently long over the entire body. It is usually most profuse on the hindquarters, although young Angoras look very much like short-coated individuals at first, with their longer coat only developing as they grow older.

Only choose a Long-haired hamster if you are prepared to groom your pet, to prevent its hair from becoming matted. This needs to be carried out gently, however, because the fur itself is quite fine and can be damaged quite easily. It is often recommended to keep these particular hamsters on paper bedding rather than shavings, as this is far less likely to become caught up and matted in the coat.

Satins

It is quite possible to combine one or more of the coat variants together in a single individual, and the combination of the Satin and Long-haired characteristics 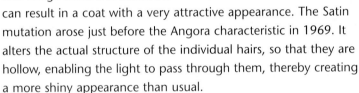 can result in a coat with a very attractive appearance. The Satin mutation arose just before the Angora characteristic in 1969. It alters the actual structure of the individual hairs, so that they are hollow, enabling the light to pass through them, thereby creating a more shiny appearance than usual.

❖ *Cinnamon Satin Syrian*

Satins are not paired together because this will lead to a thinning of the coat in their offspring so, instead, they are mated with other hamsters. This should still generally result in a number of their offspring also having satin coats, because this characteristic is genetically dominant.

Rexes

Rex Syrian Hamsters have attracted relatively little attention since this mutation cropped up in 1970. This is possibly because the early Rexes had very thin coats, which looked unattractive but, today, breeders have achieved a rather appealing and distinctive coat texture in such hamsters. The Rex mutation causes the long guard hairs in the coat to be much shorter than usual. This creates a wavy pattern, even affecting the whiskers, which are modified body hairs. Such hamsters can be bred in any colour, representing a challenge for breeders.

CHAPTER
TWO

DWARF RUSSIAN COLOUR VARIETIES

As these hamsters have become increasingly popular over recent years, so the number of recognised colour forms has increased rapidly, especially in the case of Campbell's. The natural colour of these particular Dwarf Hamsters is brownish-grey with a slate blue undercoat and a prominent black dorsal stripe, running down the centre of the back. Their underparts are a contrasting shade of white, with three streaks of brownish-grey fur protruding down each side of the body into the white fur. These areas are sometimes described as arches.

❖ Cinnamon
Campbell's

Satin Campbell's

The Satin-coated mutation was the first to be recorded, in 1985, arising in England. Just as with the same mutation in the Syrian, such hamsters have more shiny coats but, unfortunately in this case, it can also give them a rather unattractive greasy appearance, although this is not reflected in the coat's texture. Satin Campbell's can be bred in any colour.

Campbell's Opal

This is one of the better-known colour mutations, being a diluted form of the normal, first developed in the United States. The black areas in the coat are modified to a bluish-grey.

❖ Chocolate
Campbell's

Argente Campbell's

This is the most striking colour form. It has ginger-coloured fur on the top of the body, with a brownish-grey dorsal stripe, while the undercoat is bluish-grey and the underparts are ivory. The eyes are pink although there is also a Black-eyed form of the Argente, sometimes referred to as the Sandy, currently being developed in the United States. The introduction of the dark umbrous gene into Argente lineage has recently led to the creation of the Copper variety, distinguished by its burnt orange coat coloration and greyish underparts.

❖ Black Campbell's

❖ Cinnamon Platinum Campbell's

Albino and Mottled

Pink eyes are a feature of Albino Campbell's, which are easily recognisable by their pure, snow-white coats. Their ears, too, are pink, owing to the lack of colour pigment. Mottled varieties are well established, and they can be bred in any colour, with white areas predominating in their fur. This was achieved by crossing the original Patched mutation with the Albino, which increased the proportion of white fur significantly. The markings of Mottled hamsters are all highly individual. However, it is not recommended to pair them together because of a genetic weakness affecting the eyes.

❖ Cinnamon Mottled Campbell's

**CHAPTER
TWO**

Newer colours

These include the Platinum mutation, which has extensive white ticking on the upper part of its coat, creating the impression of this precious metal, while the underparts are white. The colour of these hamsters generally becomes paler with age. This feature is even more pronounced in the case of the Dilute Platinums, which can appear as Black-eyed Whites.

❖ *Mottled Agouti Campbell's*

On the other hand, there is now also a Black form which is much darker in colour than normal, with a solid black dorsal stripe. This is of European origin, having first been imported to the United Kingdom from the Netherlands in 1998. The original examples were greyer than those being bred today, but there are still small areas of white often apparent on the chin and paws.

With these varieties already in existence, there is already plenty of scope to establish further colours, such as Blue, derived from Black and Opal stock, or Dove, by pairings involving Black and Argente individuals. There is also the possibility of further mutations cropping up, creating perhaps Long-haired or Tortoiseshell forms.

❖ *Black Mottled Campbell's (new colour)*

Winter White Dwarf Russian

The Winter White form of the Dwarf Russian can undergo a dramatic change in colour. For the warmer months of the year, these hamsters are similar to Campbell's in appearance, although slightly paler. Their underparts should be whitish, although the blue tinge of their undercoat may sometimes show through here. At the onset of winter, however, these hamsters moult, often becoming entirely white, apart from the dorsal stripe down their back, which is retained. This helps to provide camouflage in the wild when there is likely to be snow on the ground, although some may have a mottled rather than a pure white appearance.

❖ *Winter White adolescent*

The coat, as with Campbell's, is thick and has an attractive woolly feel to the dense undercoat. The first colour mutation of the Winter White appeared during 1988 in the United Kingdom, and has since become known as the Sapphire. These hamsters can be distinguished by their bluish-grey coats, with the dorsal stripe also being transformed to blue. Individuals that have a pure white rather than an ivory belly are sometimes referred to as Imperials.

❖ *Winter White*

❖ *Pearl Winter White*

In 1989, the popular Pearl mutation of the Winter White arose. These hamsters are primarily white but their coat is shot through with darker black ticking. This must be even to create consistent coloration. The dorsal stripe is retained and, unusually, the Pearl has proved to be a dominant mutation. Therefore it has been possible to increase their numbers rapidly.

ROBOROVSKI'S HAMSTER

These hamsters are significantly smaller than the other Dwarf Russians, and they can also be distinguished by their longer fur. This does not lie sleek as a result, but appears slightly ruffled. Roborovski's are golden-brown in colour, with a grey undercoat. The underparts are white, and there is no dark dorsal stripe. A further point of distinction is that the division between the coloured and white areas of fur on the sides of the body is almost straight, with no sharp vertical

❖ *Roborovski's Hamster*

projections extending into the white areas. Although no variants have occurred as yet in the case of Roborovski's Hamster, it will surely only be a matter of time before colour or coat mutations are recorded in this case.

❖ *A two to three week-old Roborovski's*

CHINESE HAMSTER

This particular species is easily distinguished from the other hamsters kept as pets by the length of its tail. Chinese Hamsters actually belong to a different group, often described by zoologists as Rat-tailed Hamsters for this reason. In terms of coloration, they are naturally brown in colour with black ticking, and they also have a blackish dorsal stripe. The underparts, as in other hamsters, are significantly paler, being ivory in colour.

The Dominant Spot mutation is well-established, after being reported in 1981 from a colony of Chinese Hamsters kept at the University of Birmingham in the UK. The patterning in this case is quite variable, with white patches being evident on their upperparts, which can run together in some cases to create broader white areas. In show stock, a white spot on the head is considered desirable. Occasionally, the Dominant Spot mutation results in almost entirely white individuals being bred, although these are not desirable for exhibition purposes, where even patches and spotting is preferred.

Much more scarce at present are pure White Chinese Hamsters, which first appeared in Switzerland. This change has been shown to be a recessive characteristic, in contrast to the Dominant Spot, confirming that it is a separate mutation. The dorsal stripe is still evident in the case of the White Chinese, with the eyes again being black. Again, there is every possibility that further new colours or coat variants are likely to occur in the case of the Chinese Hamster in the future.

❖ *Chinese Hamster*

CHAPTER THREE

Behaviour
and biology

Although hamsters have been kept as pets for decades now,
they still retain many of the behavioural characteristics of their
wild ancestors. This helps to explain why they hoard food in
their sleeping accommodation and will rapidly disappear out of
sight in a room if they escape from their quarters.

H amsters are rodents, and so display many of the
characteristics of this large group of mammals.
Foremost among these is a very powerful set of incisor
teeth at the front of their mouths. The description of 'rodent'
actually comes from the Latin word *rodere*, meaning 'to gnaw'.
Rodents rely upon these teeth not only to break open the hard
casings of seeds and nuts, but also to assist
them in constructing retreats where they
will be relatively safe from predators, since
they face many threats to their survival.

▌ Sound teeth

The way in which the two incisor teeth,
which are present in both the upper
and lower jaws, meet is very important,
because if these teeth are misaligned in any

way, a hamster will have difficulty in eating and may even starve as a consequence. The outer face of the incisors is covered in hard-wearing enamel, with softer dentine behind. These substances wear away at different rates, so the incisors end up with a very sharp cutting edge like a chisel, consisting of enamel.

The incisors need to meet exactly, so that their cutting edge stays sharp, and because of the hard wear on these teeth, they continue growing throughout the hamster's life. It is very important with pet hamsters to provide them with plenty of opportunities to gnaw because otherwise their teeth can become overgrown, making it difficult for the hamster to eat.

There is a gap, called the diastema, behind the incisor teeth as hamsters do not have pointed canine teeth in their mouths like

Above: *The sharp incisor teeth of hamsters are critical for their survival in the wild, being used not just for eating but also to assist in tunnelling underground.*

humans. This space also means that a hamster can manage to gnaw without being at risk of actually swallowing inedible material, by sucking its cheeks in behind the incisor teeth. Their food is actually crushed up further back in the mouth, using the premolar and molar teeth, which have broad surfaces for this purpose.

▌Staying alive

Hamsters, like most rodents, are small in size and vulnerable to predators. Their life is often hazardous as they face many dangers, ranging from wild cats to birds of prey. Unable to defend themselves effectively from attack, they must rely mainly on remaining out of sight to stay alive. Within the confines of their burrows, hamsters will be relatively safe, but they need to emerge regularly in search of food. Water is less of a problem because dew may form at the burrow's entrance, and roots entering here can also help to meet their fluid requirement.

Hamsters also conceal their presence by remaining in their burrows during the daytime, emerging to seek food as dusk

▌**Right:** *Even in captivity, pet hamsters like to burrow into their nest bedding and will emerge for food or drink, or to gnaw on wood or play on their wheel.*

CHAPTER
THREE

Above: *Hamsters often stuff their cheek pouches with food, and this makes their faces appear to be swollen.*

falls. This behaviour still remains common in domestic strains, after hundreds of generations, but in the wild it gives no certainty of safety. The longer that a hamster is out of its burrow, then the more vulnerable it is to being attacked, which makes feeding above ground a hazardous occupation.

A further threat to their survival is the fact that many species, such as the Syrian, live in relatively arid parts of the world, where food may not be freely available throughout the year, and so they could be at risk from starvation. In order to minimize these dangers, hamsters are able to carry large amounts of food back to their burrows quickly and efficiently, building up stores here which can be eaten later. The amount of food taken underground has led to hamsters being regarded as agricultural pests in some areas. As an example, the Common Hamster (*Cricetus cricetus*) has been known to accumulate stores of as much as 90 kg (198 lb) of food in its burrows.

Pouches and paws

Hamsters take food back to their burrows by filling special pouches in their mouths. These are basically folds within the cheeks, which extend back in the mouth as far as the shoulders. The hamster uses its front paws like hands to pick up items of food, which it then stuffs into its pouches, carrying them back to its burrow. The pouches are then emptied, with the food being added to the hamster's store if it is not immediately eaten. Domestic hamsters behave in a similar way, frequently accumulating a supply. The hamster's front paws are quite flexible and, apart from handling food, they are also used for washing and grooming purposes. A hamster will often sit up on its hindquarters when cleaning itself, as this makes the task easier, allowing it not just to wipe its face but also to groom its underparts. Hamsters may also adopt this posture when they detect an unfamiliar scent, such as the presence of another

Right: *Grooming is a very important part of a hamster's daily routine. Even so, you will need to help in the case of a long-haired hamster.*

Right: *Hamsters can easily support their weight on their hindquarters, standing in this way.*

hamster nearby, as this gives them a better view of their immediate environment.

Keeping in touch

Unlike many rodents, Syrian Hamsters, in particular, are anti-social by nature, living in burrows on their own. This is often a feature of animals in desert areas, where food resources may be scarce. They are quiet animals, relying mainly on scent for communication purposes. They possess a keen sense of smell and special scent glands on their bodies to mark their burrows.

These so-called 'hip spots' are symmetrical and show up as dark areas on the skin. They are most obvious in male hamsters, especially during the breeding period, and they may lick these areas, causing the fur here to appear damp, or even fall out in some cases, as the result of persistent grooming. This is usually only temporary, however, and any lost hair should soon grow back. Dwarf Russian Hamsters also have another scent gland on the underside of their body, in the midline, known as a ventral scent gland. The secretions produced by this gland can be used to mark objects that the hamster climbs over.

Hamsters also have relatively large, prominent eyes, which enable them to see reasonably well under conditions of relative darkness. The whiskers on their faces are specially-adapted, thickened sensory hairs which help to provide information about their environment at close quarters, by detecting vibrations in the wind or by directly coming into contact with objects.

Remaining hidden

The natural coloration of hamsters helps to provide them with camouflage, especially when they are viewed from above. For instance, the sandy appearance of the Syrian Hamster enables it to blend in against its background, whereas the coat change of the Winter White serves to conceal its presence in the wintertime when there is likely to be snow on the ground.

The paler underparts of all the hamsters covered in this book may serve to reflect heat from their bodies, since areas of the world where they are found can become very hot at times, leaving them potentially vulnerable to heat stress (see page 126).

Hamsters rely mainly on their legs to construct their burrows, although they will also use their incisor teeth to grasp stones, even carrying them up to the entrance of the burrow in this way. Although their front paws are important for tunnelling and digging away at the soil with their claws, it is actually the hind legs that are used to push the soil out of the burrow. The burrows themselves consist of a series of chambers, which are linked by connecting tunnels.

Unlike some rodents, hamsters cannot jump well, although their powerful hindquarters do allow them to climb without too much difficulty. They are not as agile as some other rodents, such as mice, however, which use their long tails both to maintain their balance and even to grip on to objects to prevent themselves from falling when they are climbing off the ground.

Right: *The eyes of hamsters are relatively large, as in the case of many rodents which are active after dusk.*

CHAPTER
THREE

Hamsters in the wild

In spite of being able to retreat underground to escape from danger, hamsters generally have a relatively short lifespan, but they compensate for this by breeding fast. This, in turn, means that their numbers can grow rapidly when the environmental conditions are favourable.

Surprisingly little has been documented about the populations of hamsters in the wild, although it is known that the so-called Common Hamster, which is a large species, weighing over 500 g (17 oz) has disappeared over recent years from many of the former areas where it used to be quite numerous.

The Syrian is thought to be both rare and localized in its area of distribution around Mount Aleppo, although since these rodents live several metres below the surface, it is not easy for researchers to gain an accurate impression of their numbers. Their secretive, nocturnal natures mean that studies are difficult to carry out,

Below: *Although the hamster's natural coloration appears attractive, it has evolved to conceal the presence of these rodents.*

Above: *Hamsters spend relatively long periods asleep. Curling up in a ball helps to conserve their body heat.*

especially over an area of any size. This same problem applies particularly when trying to assess the numbers of Dwarf Russian and Chinese Hamsters, especially as, like many small rodents, their population numbers may also fluctuate quite dramatically over the course of a number of years as the result of various environmental factors.

It is not even clear whether hamsters regularly hibernate in the wild although, certainly, such behaviour can occur in pet hamsters during the winter if they are housed in cold environments. The colour change that has been noted in the Winter White suggests that such behaviour is not common, however, because if these small mammals spent most of the winter months sleeping snugly in an underground nest, there would be little purpose in developing a coat that corresponded in colour to the landscape above.

CHAPTER FOUR

Acquiring a hamster

Deciding which hamster to choose can be a difficult decision, and this is not something that should be rushed. After all, your hamster will be part of your daily life for hopefully two years or longer, which means that it is especially important to make the right choice at the outset.

T he first thing that you will need to decide is which type of hamster appeals to you most. Unfortunately, it is not generally possible to keep the different types of hamster together successfully, although members of the same species, Winter Whites and Campbell's, could be housed in this way. This is not recommended, however, because their distinctive characteristics will be lost if they breed successfully, while their offspring may be infertile, and you are likely to have difficulty in finding homes for young pups from such pairings.

If you are interested in colour-breeding and showing, the greatest potential in these areas exists in the case of the Syrian at present, although there is growing scope within Campbell's Dwarf Russians, thanks to the increasing number of colour forms that are now available. Roborovski's Hamster has a reputation for being slightly shyer than the other Dwarf Russians and therefore is perhaps less suitable if you want to have a very tame hamster.

As far as children's pets are concerned, the other Dwarf

Right: *Dwarf Russians are relatively social by nature and can be kept in small groups, unlike Syrian Hamsters.*

Russians are a good choice, because they can prove to be relatively social, which can reduce the housing costs slightly, should you have more than one child seeking a pet hamster. Chinese Hamsters are unusual and have a very distinctive appearance but, in this case, although two females may live together amenably, males are likely to fight and will need to be kept separately. They can become very tame though, and young Chinese Hamsters will soon start to feed readily from the hand.

Where to obtain a hamster

It is not generally difficult to acquire a hamster, especially Syrians, as they are available from many pet stores, although if you are seeking a particular colour, then you may have to be more patient and possibly find a breeder. Certainly, if you are interested in exhibiting hamsters in due course, then it is important to start with quality stock from winning bloodlines. There are likely to be significant differences in appearance between hamsters that are being sold as pets and those of exhibition quality, and this, in turn, means that an ordinary pet hamster is unlikely to win its class when entered in a show.

The importance of age

Perhaps the most important thing, however, particularly when seeking a pet, is to choose a young hamster. This will ensure that you can tame your hamster far more easily and also enjoy its companionship for as long as possible, since they are quite short-lived pets, with a typical life expectancy of two or three years. In the case of Dwarf Russian and Chinese Hamsters, which may live together within their own groups, it is much better to start out with young individuals, preferably nestmates. There should then be no conflict when placing them in new surroundings, whereas, at the other extreme, trying to introduce two older individuals together is likely to be fraught with danger.

Hamsters are normally weaned by the time they are just over three weeks old and, in the case of those with patterned markings, their appearance will not alter significantly throughout their lives. The coats of Angora Syrians will, however, become longer. In

Below: *It is always best to choose a young hamster rather than an older individual, partly because they are easier to tame at this early stage in life.*

terms of assessing the overall show potential of a hamster, however, you may be better to wait until the hamster is between seven and 12 weeks old, by which time it is easier to see how closely its physical appearance, or 'type', is likely to correspond to that which is required for exhibition purposes.

Starting out with exhibition hamsters

It helps if you are able to visit a number of shows before setting out to buy any stock, so that you can gain an insight into the hamsters that are winning, and what the judges are looking for, when determining the placings in a class. This will also give you the opportunity to meet breeders. The Internet provides the simplest way to start a search for clubs and breeders, and by

Above: *A litter of young Syrian Hamsters will be weaned and ready to go to new homes when they are a month old.*

The value of paperwork

Record-keeping is a very important part of maintaining a hamster stud, enabling you to trace the ancestry of individuals and plan out your breeding programme. Good record-keeping is therefore vital for this purpose, and when you are purchasing exhibition stock, you will not only need to know the date of the hamster's birth but, hopefully, you will also receive a pedigree which sets out its ancestry as well. It should extend back over three generations or more, giving information such as the colours of these hamsters, along with their patterning and coat types. This information can help to explain how unexpected features sometimes crop up in bloodlines, as well as assisting you in planning your own breeding programmes in due course.

finding out the details of clubs in your area, you can soon obtain details of local shows as well. Alternatively, you may be able to find this information from newsstand magazines covering pets, or possibly at your local reference library.

Arrange with the breeder a convenient time to call, then, hopefully, it will be possible to see the stud of hamsters, including the breeder's top specimens, at close quarters. This can be invaluable in helping you to gain an insight into the desirable features, which you will need to develop in your own hamsters in due

Right: New colour variants are still being bred, as shown by this Chinese Hamster. Colour varieties in this species are still quite scarce.

course. But do not expect to be able to buy the best hamsters on view, as these are unlikely to be for sale. You would be better to follow the advice of the breeder and choose younger specimens, which are closely-related to the winning bloodlines. These are most likely to give rise to top-quality offspring in due course.

There is always the possibility that you may be able to acquire an older hamster who has previously been very successful at shows, and this is well worth considering in the case of a male. You will hopefully be able to use him successfully to mate with a young female, as a foundation for your stud. Place particular emphasis on the quality of the hamsters you are choosing at the outset, and start on a small scale because you are likely to find that your stud grows rapidly, thanks to the hamster's prolific nature.

Male or female?

Sexing hamsters when they are weaned is usually relatively straightforward, although the differences between the sexes will become more pronounced as a result of sexual maturity. You will need to pick up the hamster or possibly just transfer it to a carrying container with a clear base, so that you can view its underparts easily. The gap between the anus and the genital opening is very much shorter in the case of a female hamster, compared with a male. In the case of a mature male, the testes will be apparent under the skin as bulges on either side of the tail.

It is also possible to sex hamsters at this stage by viewing them from the side.

■ Females have a much more rounded and smooth body contour extending from the end of the back down to the tail.

■ That of male hamsters is more step-like in appearance because of the presence of their testes. These are especially evident in male Chinese Hamsters.

■ In the case of mature hamsters, you are also likely to notice a

Above: *Syrian Hamsters can be sexed from their body profile once they are mature.*

Above: *A female hamster for comparison. In youngsters, the ano-genital gap is used for sexing purposes.*

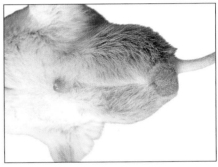

Above: *Mature male hamsters have very large testes, relative to their body size, as in this Chinese.*

variation in size between the sexes, with the females growing larger than the males.

There are no significant differences in temperament between the sexes so, especially if you are seeking a Syrian hamster as a pet, there is little need to worry about its gender. But if you are interested in exhibiting, then it is better to have more females than males. This will give you greater flexibility in your breeding

CHAPTER
FOUR

Above: *Never hold a hamster tightly in your hand, as this is likely to cause it to bite you. This applies especially in the case of hamsters that are not used to being handled regularly.*

programme, since you can arrange for a female to be mated with another male kept by a fellow enthusiast.

In the case of Dwarf Russian Hamsters, however, gender can be much more significant, as these hamsters may be kept in groups. Females tend to be less quarrelsome in these surroundings than males, and clearly you need to be sure of the sexes under these circumstances to prevent unwanted litters. There is also a risk that should you buy a female which has been kept as part of

Checklist

Before buying a hamster, examine it carefully and look out for the following points:

- The eyes should be bright with no tear staining.
- There must be no bald or thin patches of fur.
- The ears must not be torn or damaged.
- There should be no scars on the body.
- Ensure there is no staining on the fur around the vent.
- The hamster should have no difficulty in moving.
- The fur ought to be quite sleek, depending on the coat type.
- Be sure that the claws and paws are not injured in any way.

Above: Check a hamster before purchasing it to ensure that it has no obvious health problems.

a mixed sex group, there is a slight possibility that she could already be pregnant by the age of 10 weeks. In the case of Chinese Hamsters, you will need to be sure that you only choose true pairs or females which you wish to house in groups, because of the likely aggression of males towards each other.

CHAPTER
FOUR

A final decision

Having made your provisional choice, ask the vendor to pick up the hamster so you can look at it more closely. This will give you the opportunity to spot any problems that may have been less obvious when the hamster was in its quarters, especially if it was partly concealed in its nest. You will also be able to gain some insight into how tame the hamster is, particularly if it is already active. Bear in mind, however, that a sleepy hamster roused from its bed will be less likely to attempt to run off and therefore may appear to be tamer than, in fact, is the case. There is, of course, nothing to stop you handling the hamster with the owner's permission, but it is more likely to be frightened under these circumstances and so could decide to bite, simply because your scent will be unfamiliar to it.

Travelling home with a hamster

It is very important not to overlook this aspect of buying a hamster, since it is not unknown for people to set out on a journey with their pet and end up at their destination with an empty box! Hamsters are great escape artists and will easily find somewhere to hide in the confines of a car, especially if they slip out of their carrier undetected. It can be very worrying and also sometimes expensive to retrieve a hamster that is loose in the interior of a vehicle.

Carrying containers

Unfortunately, some pet stores still supply cardboard carriers of the type used for small pet birds when selling hamsters. The hamster will be able to use its sharp teeth to gnaw out of the cardboard easily, often by enlarging one of the ventilation holes which serve as a convenient starting point for an escape. It is therefore much better to invest in one of the lightweight carrying containers, complete with a ventilated hood and handles, to bring your hamster home. In this case, all you need to do is simply check that the lid is firmly in place before lifting up the carrier. This container will also be very useful as a temporary receptacle for your pet when you are cleaning its quarters.

Should you be buying more than one hamster, it is better to bring them back in separate carriers, otherwise, being so closely confined, they are more likely to fight in these surroundings with devastating consequences. If possible, line the carrier with bedding so that your hamster will be encouraged to settle down more readily on the journey.

Travelling tips

It is better to keep the hamster on the floor in a shaded area of the car on the way home. Never be tempted to put it in the boot, because of the risk of exhaust fumes penetrating into this compartment, which are likely to prove deadly for your new pet. Also, try to avoid breaking your journey home. Do not be tempted to leave your hamster in the car while you pop off to do some shopping, because in spite of coming from parts of the world where the temperature can be very hot, hamsters are vulnerable to heat stroke. They will die quickly if left in a locked car, as the temperature in the vehicle can rise to a fatal level for them within minutes. Normally, hamsters can avoid the sun when it is at its hottest, simply by remaining within their burrows, which help to insulate them from extremes of temperature.

Right: *Hamsters are great escape artists, thanks partly to their sharp teeth, so invest in a secure carrier for your pet.*

CHAPTER FIVE

Housing

Keeping a hamster in the home has never been easier, with a
wide choice of housing options now available. But do not get
too carried away simply with the style of the hamster's home;
remember that space for exercise and ease of cleanliness are
more important practical considerations when you are
deciding how best to house your new pet.

There are a number of ways in which you can house your hamster, depending partly on the type of hamster you have chosen. If possible, it is a good idea to decide on the most suitable type of accommodation before actually acquiring your hamster, so that you can have everything set up in advance for your new pet. This is important because it may be advisable to wash the hamster's quarters, especially if you are using a converted aquarium, which may not only be dusty but may also contain small spicules of glass in the base, which could possibly harm your pet.

Right: *It is usually better to obtain your hamster after you have acquired its home.*

Hamster cages

There is a wide range of different designs of hamster cage now available, and it is better to choose a relatively spacious, tiered model which incorporates ladders for climbing and platforms where the hamster can sit. Such units offer more space than a conventional cage, which restricts the hamster to the floor area and climbing around the bars. Modern hamster cages are usually comprised of a plastic base unit which detaches easily from the top wire component, making them quite easy to clean and wash out at intervals as required.

Above: *A lightweight plastic (acrylic) enclosure with a ventilated lid. Fitting toys here can be difficult.*

Check the way in which the base unit is attached in place, however, as this can be a point of weakness in some cases. The top section should slide over it on all sides, so that it is kept securely in place. Beware of units held together by

Right: *This style of cage with horizontal bars will allow your hamster to climb around its home. Check the strength of the clips holding the base in place.*

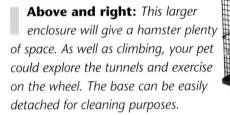

Above and right: *This larger enclosure will give a hamster plenty of space. As well as climbing, your pet could explore the tunnels and exercise on the wheel. The base can be easily detached for cleaning purposes.*

plastic clips. These invariably weaken and may break over a period of time, with the risk that the cage will fall apart, which could result in your pet suffering a fatal fall. There is also the problem of obtaining spare parts for cages if you need to replace these fitments, which can sometimes be surprisingly difficult.

Tubular systems

It is much easier to obtain new sections in the case of tubular systems, which have become a popular way of accommodating hamsters over recent years. Many people start off by purchasing a starter kit and then add extra parts to it, giving the hamster a larger area and more sections to explore. The concept behind these units is that they more closely resemble the hamster's natural way of living, in a series of tunnels and chambers. Great flexibility exists within these housing kits, as they can be

Below: *Tubular housing systems are now available in a range of styles. Generally, you buy a starter kit and then add new sections to it, but cleaning this style of accommodation is often more difficult than with a cage.*

assembled in a variety of configurations, and younger owners especially like to redesign their hamster's living quarters. It is important, however, to ensure that there is no risk of the rodent disappearing into the room while this is being carried out.

Being made of bright colours and translucent plastic, these tubular housing systems look striking and also allow the hamster to be seen at all times, as it trundles through the network of tunnels, building up a foodstore in a chamber or sleeping.

Right: *The different components for tubular housing systems can be bought easily. However, replacement clips for cages, to hold the base in place, can be harder to acquire.*

Security considerations

Tubular systems are quite easy to clean, although it is not a good idea to wash them in boiling water, because this may not only cause them to become more opaque but also can distort the connections. This type of damage can then become a weakness, because an accessible edge of plastic will be no match for the hamster's sharp incisor teeth. It will soon be able to gnaw its way out under these circumstances, usually at night, so always keep a watch for any signs of such damage.

This also applies to the plastic-based cages, because if there is a significant gap between the two components, then a pet hamster may decide to exercise its teeth determinedly in this

Above: *Cats can represent an obvious danger to hamsters in the home, and this is another reason why it is vital that your pet's housing is really secure.*

CHAPTER
FIVE

Buying a second-hand hamster home

You may be able to pick up a second-hand cage quite easily, often through the columns of local newspapers. These can represent something of a bargain, since often, they will only have been home to a hamster for a couple of years and will be in very good condition. If possible, try to discover the fate of the previous occupant, because if it passed away prematurely then it could have been suffering from an illness rather than dying from natural causes.

It is also important to look for signs of wear, such as a gnawed base or some rust. This can be very harmful because if the rust particles are swallowed, they are likely to upset the hamster's digestive system. Flaky or bubbling paintwork on the base may be an indicator of rust beneath. If you are offered one of the older-style cages with a metal base, look carefully in the corners, because this is where rust is most likely to be apparent.

Any actual holes are not only potentially dangerous for the hamster, which could cut its foot or leg on the sharp edges, but will also mean that its bedding will fall out of the cage. Being made of folded metal, it is important to check that none of the edges have become raised, as these, too, can be sharp. It should be possible to fold them back again into place, but take care not to damage the paintwork as this can lead to rusting.

Cleanliness

When purchasing second-hand hamster housing without an existing occupant, be sure to wash and disinfect it thoroughly, allowing it to dry before acquiring another hamster. Use one of the special disinfectant products now stocked by most pet stores and recommended for cleaning small mammal housing, following the instructions on the packaging carefully, to ensure that its germicidal power is maximized. You will then need to rinse off the components thoroughly, so as to remove all trace of the disinfectant, before reassembling the cage.

area of its accommodation, especially if it has nothing else to gnaw in its quarters.

The door fastening can also be an area of weakness in some cages. Over a period of time, this can work loose or, if sprung, the door may not fall back properly closed, leaving a gap through which your pet could escape into the room. It may be advisable to invest in a small padlock, operating on a combination code rather than a key, which will allow you to be sure that the door stays securely closed.

Housing Dwarf Russian Hamsters

These hamsters tend not to be kept in the conventional cages designed for their Syrian relatives, because of their smaller size. This applies especially in the case of young individuals which may slip through the mesh of these cages, or could end up being trapped here instead. A better option for housing them is therefore a converted aquarium, with a secure and well-ventilated hood. There are also much larger versions of the basic acrylic carrying pen which can be suitable.

The drawback of using an aquarium is that it will probably be made of glass, which will be heavy to move for cleaning purposes and smashes readily if dropped. Should you opt for one of the basic tanks held together simply with silicone rubber sealant, without an overlaying plastic surround, you must take particular care when lifting the unit. There could be sharp edges of glass out of sight underneath, which may inflict a painful gash on your hand.

Right: *The relatively small size of Dwarf Russian Hamsters must be considered when housing them.*

CHAPTER
FIVE

Tank covers

Obtaining a suitable cover for this type of set-up can be difficult, because a fish tank hood is unlikely to give adequate ventilation, whereas a tank cover of the type sold for reptiles will almost inevitably have a large hole for a light fitting. You will need to be sure that a hamster will not be able to climb up on a piece of decor and then clamber out through this space. Therefore the

Above: *Floor space is important for hamsters. They must be able to move around here, have somewhere to sleep and also possibly a wheel which will allow them to exercise.*

best option may be to place a heavy plant pot or an ornament on the top of the tank cover to hide this hole.

One distinct advantage of choosing a hood of this type is that there is a simple sliding door giving good access to the interior and which will allow you to lift hamsters in and out easily. These hoods are constructed in such a way that they fit snugly over the top of the sides of the tank and cannot be accidentally dislodged by other pets. They are available in a wide range of sizes, so that you can keep your hamsters in a large area, which lessens the likelihood of fighting if you want to house them in a group, although they should all be introduced at the same time; any newcomer is likely to be badly persecuted.

The third possibility is to make a suitable hood, using 19 gauge 1.25 cm (^{1}/$_2$ in) square mesh, attaching this to a timber framework of similar dimensions, which also fits down over the side of the tank. By placing horizontal wooden bars across the top, you can incorporate a hinged door, allowing you to reach into the tank without the inconvenience of having to lift off the top. A door of this type also acts as a security aid, because if the entire top is left open and you are momentarily distracted by something else in the home, this could make it easier for a cat to seize the hamsters.

It is relatively hard to acquire acrylic aquaria of any size, and their sides may sometimes discolour over a period of time, as well as scratching easily compared with glass. However, they are easy to move. If you opt for a plastic pet carrier-design, choose the largest available model. Although lightweight, the moulding means that there are no edges that will allow hamsters to gnaw their way out. Take care not to drop the unit, however, because the acrylic can break quite easily, and always check that the lid has clicked back firmly into place after it is lifted off. The entry point here is quite narrow, so you will probably need to remove the lid itself in order to pick up your hamster easily.

CHAPTER
FIVE

Bedding

There are various types of bedding that are suitable for your hamster. However, never use sawdust. The fine particles are likely to irritate your hamster's eyes and nose, leading to inflammation of the eyes, and they can cause repeated sneezing as well. The traditional floor covering is coarse wooden shavings, but be certain only to use those sold in pet shops, which are packaged for use as animal bedding. Even though these are free from harmful preservatives, there are worries associated with both pine and cedar shavings, because of the natural resins in these woods. It is believed that these may be absorbed into the hamster's body, affecting its liver.

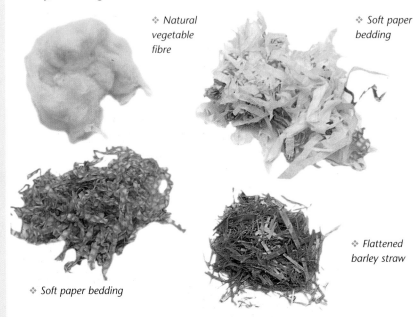

❖ *Natural vegetable fibre*

❖ *Soft paper bedding*

❖ *Soft paper bedding*

❖ *Flattened barley straw*

Above: *Always choose one of the special types of hamster bedding which are now widely-sold. These will be safe for your pet, since they should not cause any intestinal obstruction if swallowed.*

Right: *Hamsters will always move their bedding around, sometimes piling it up in the entrance to their house.*

As a result of such concerns, more hamster-keepers are starting to use other types of bedding. Various forms of special paper bedding have become popular, being used to form a lining on the floor of the hamster's quarters, while special soft, flattened lengths of barley straw are another possibility, being sold in packets for this purpose.

Note: It is very important to ensure that only safe bedding is used, because otherwise this is likely to be swallowed and can

Below: *Packeted wood shavings are the traditional choice as a floor covering in a hamster's cage.*

CHAPTER
FIVE

Above: *Tease out your hamster's bedding before placing it in its house, as it will have been compacted in its packaging.*

cause a fatal blockage in the hamster's intestinal tract. Even shavings, for example, may stick readily to slices of apple and end up being inadvertently swallowed as a result.

Sleeping quarters

It is very important to provide a suitable retreat for a hamster where it can sleep during the day. There are a number of different options available for this purpose, and your choice is likely to be influenced in part by the space available. A simple plastic house with an entry hole will soon be adopted by a hamster, which will make a nest here. The plastic can be washed easily, and generally will not be gnawed, especially if you provide your pet with special chews to exercise its teeth. It is easy to

Right: *Nests of this type are just one of the many* options for a hamster's sleeping quarters, which are available from pet stores.

keep the interior of such houses clean, since the roof lifts off to give easy access. Another possibility is smaller cube-shaped structures, which are ideal for Dwarf Russian Hamsters, providing them with snug sleeping quarters.

Even if you are using another type of bedding on the floor of the hamster's quarters, some paper or another type of soft-fibre bedding should be provided as a nest where it can sleep. Again, for safety's sake, only use material supplied for this purpose. Otherwise, not only may the hamster swallow unsuitable bedding, but it could end up being trapped by it. For example, if it wraps around a leg.

Do not worry if your hamster chooses to rearrange its bed occasionally – this is quite

Left: *Hamsters always like to investigate all the objects in* their quarters, even if they decide not to sleep in them.

CHAPTER
FIVE

Right: *Tubular systems
usually incorporate a larger
section, intended as sleeping
quarters for the hamster.*

normal. During the warmer summer
months, it may decide to push some
of the material out of its house, even creating a bed in
the corner of its quarters and preferring to sleep here for a time.

Bedding in tubular systems

It is usually only recommended to provide a lining in those areas
of the system where the hamster is likely to spend time, such as
the sleeping quarters. Do not be surprised, however, if your pet
moves its bedding around between various sections of its housing,
as this is quite normal behaviour.

Toys

The traditional wheel is still highly favoured, particularly for
Syrian hamsters. If possible, always choose a closed design of
wheel so that there is no risk of your
hamster's leg accidentally slipping
through the runners and becoming

Left: *Plastic is used in
the design of many
hamster toys, but it can
be damaged by teeth.*

Left: *A wooden log serves both as
a toy and somewhere your hamster
can safely exercise its teeth.*

Above: *A wooden see-saw. Like other toys, this will need to be scrubbed clean on occasions, and left to dry before being placed back in the hamster's quarters.*

Above: *Wheels are very popular toys for hamsters, but even those of plastic design can be very noisy if they are not mounted correctly. Enclosed wheels are the safest choice.*

caught up here as it pedals round. Some cages come equipped with wheels, while there are also free-standing designs available which can be fitted into converted aquaria without difficulty. There are also wheels that are incorporated into sections for tubular housing systems.

Toys are important for the following reasons:

■ They serve to keep your hamster fit and active
■ They assist in preventing it from becoming overweight
■ They can help to prolong its life.

It is often difficult to predict which toys are likely to appeal most to your hamster, as they do have individual preferences. Some like wooden see-saws and similar toys, such as those of tubular design which they can scurry through. When it comes to selecting toys, do not overcrowd your pet's quarters. You may want to rotate them, however, so that your hamster will have a varying range of toys to choose from, rather than just being restricted to just one or two.

Below: *Household items, such as cardboard tubes from paper towels, are also often appreciated by hamsters.*

CHAPTER
FIVE

Outdoor housing

If you decide to expand your interest in hamsters, then it may be necessary to set up separate accommodation for them outdoors in a suitable outbuilding such as a shed. A structure of this type can usually be converted quite easily to meet their needs, although it can be advantageous for it to have an electricity supply. This work should be undertaken by a qualified electrician to ensure that it will be safe and complies with the legal requirements. A light fitting will be very useful, and you may also want to be able to heat the interior during cold spells, or even run a fan during the summer to cool the interior of the building.

The importance of insulation

It is actually very important to insulate the structure well, as this will help to restrict temperature fluctuations throughout the year. Excessive heat is actually just as dangerous for hamsters as cold weather. Insulation quilt can make a significant difference if used to fill up the roof spaces and the sides of the shed. It can be boarded in by sheets of either thin plywood or oil-tempered hardboard, held in place with panel pins attaching to the framework of the shed. Always read and follow the instructions carefully when working with this material, as it can be potentially hazardous. Once the interior is lined, then this can be painted, preferably with a light-coloured emulsion paint.

You can also add secondary double-glazing, plus draught insulators around the door, which should help to keep the temperature of the building more constant. If you need to provide additional heating, then a tubular heater of the type sold for use in greenhouses is the safest option. This will be enclosed in a safety cage of mesh, and the cabling too should be protected, particularly in case a hamster escapes from its quarters. Fitting a thermostat is recommended, so as to minimize heating costs.

Fluorescent strip lighting can be useful, particularly in temperate areas, so that you will be able to look after your hamsters when the days are short during the winter. There are different types of such lighting, and it is preferable to choose one with wavelengths corresponding to that of natural daylight, since this can help you to carry out a more accurate assessment of your hamsters' coloration. Some breeders also incorporate an ionizer in their hamstery, which helps to reduce the level of dust in the atmosphere and can also kill off any harmful microbes being wafted around on the air currents, thereby reducing the risk of disease.

Equipping the interior

The hamster cages themselves should be supported on shelving, held in place securely with brackets, at a convenient height so that you can see into the cages easily. If you are arranging a double-tier of cages, then be sure to allow sufficient space so that if the door opening is in the top of the cage, you can reach in to the interior easily. It also helps to have a table where you can place the cages for cleaning purposes.

Food should be stored in metal bins to deter wild rodents from invading the shed, and possibly spreading disease to the hamsters as a result. The bins can be located under the table, to maximize the use of space in the shed.

Always avoid placing the cages in such a position that they are likely to be in bright sunlight, especially not directly in front of a window, because the temperature in this area may rise very sharply on a warm day. If this is a risk, then it is a good idea to arrange for the windows to open, although take care to ensure this will not in turn create a draught. You should also ensure that the area in front of the windows is covered with mesh, so as to prevent any risk of a cat slipping in and disturbing, if not actually harming, the hamsters.

CHAPTER SIX

Looking after your hamster

Even if you have a busy lifestyle, caring for a hamster will not take up a lot of time, allowing you to enjoy the company of your pet rather than having to spend long periods attending to its needs. Hamsters also make relatively inexpensive companions, with their feeding costs being low.

Hamsters are quite easy pets to care for, although they will require your daily attention. One of the first things that you will need to decide is where in the home you want to keep your hamster. This will depend partly on whether you own a dog or, particularly, a cat which may seek to persecute your new pet. Since hamsters do not smell provided that they are cleaned out regularly, you could position its quarters in the living room, where you will be able to watch the hamster easily while relaxing in a chair.

 If you are using a converted aquarium for housing purposes, then there will be no risk of anything ending up outside the cage. This can sometimes happen with a traditional cage, so it is best

CHAPTER
SIX

Locations to avoid

■ A spot just in front of a window, because of the sun.
■ A location next to a stereo system or television, as the sounds may upset your pet.
■ Anywhere draughty, such as a hall.
■ Avoid the kitchen, partly because of the fumes.
■ The bathroom, because of the high humidity.
■ Anywhere with houseplants in reach of your pet, as the leaves could be poisonous.
■ An area near the floor where a dog or cat could easily reach the hamster.

stood on a surface that can be wiped over easily. Always try to position the hamster's quarters where your pet will be clearly visible and can be lifted out of its cage easily.

Settling-in

When you first transfer your new pet into its quarters, bear in mind that it is likely to be upset after its journey and therefore keep any handling to a minimum at this stage. It may actually be better to allow the hamster to climb out by itself into its new surroundings, before checking that it is secure. Many hamsters will often explore their new surroundings briefly before retreating to their sleeping quarters. They will then emerge towards dusk in search of food and water.

Food and water containers

The best type of food pot for hamsters will be a heavy earthenware pot, which is a smaller version of the type often used for dogs and cats. Their weight means that they are very difficult to tip over, so that there is no real likelihood of your hamster inadvertently depriving itself of food in this way, as could happen with lighter containers. Nor will a hamster be able to damage an earthenware food container by gnawing at its sides.

It is not a good idea to provide drinking water in this form of open container because it is likely to become soiled with bedding. Water will then be drawn out of the container by capillary action, soaking the surrounding floor area, which could be harmful for the hamster. Special drinking bottles are available for hamsters, and these can be fitted easily to the side of the cage using a loop of wire. Always check that the bottle is positioned with the spout at a convenient height for your hamster to drink from without difficulty.

With converted aquaria and acrylic enclosures, there are special wire cradles that you can use to suspend the drinking bottle firmly and securely off the roof section, allowing the hamster to drink safely. In the case of tubular housing systems, the drinker is specially designed to screw into one of the units.

The stainless steel spout used in all cases is quite resistant to the hamster's sharp teeth, and protects what are usually two movable balls within, although only one of these is visible. Always fill the drinker to the top, so that it is completely full, to create a vacuum once it is inverted. This prevents water

Right: *Earthenware food containers are ideal for hamsters as they cannot gnaw on them. When this baby hamster grows up, it will be able to feed from such a bowl.*

CHAPTER
SIX

Right: *Seeds feature prominently in the diet of hamsters. They can use their front feet like hands to hold their food.*

dribbling out of the spout and wetting the bedding beneath.

Although healthy hamsters do not drink large volumes of water, usually less than 20 ml (²/₃ fl oz) each day, a fresh supply should be supplied on a daily basis in order to safeguard their health. Otherwise, harmful bacteria may multiply in the water, upsetting your hamster's digestive system. You should always wash the drinker out thoroughly once or twice a week, especially if you are giving a vitamin and mineral supplement of any kind in the drinking water.

Clean the interior of the bottle thoroughly with a bottle brush. Otherwise, unsightly algal growth is soon likely to grow on the sides of the bottle, especially if it is located in bright light, and this can be difficult to remove completely. Be careful about using a disinfectant, however, and stick to those sold specifically for use with small mammals, rinsing the drinker thoroughly afterwards before refilling it.

Food

Hamsters feed mainly on vegetable matter of different types, especially dry seeds and nuts. There are various mixes widely available from pet stores, which will form a good basic diet for your pet. However they do vary in their ingredients, and it is probably better to buy one of the more expensive mixes, especially since hamsters only have relatively small appetites, eating just 5–7 g ($^1/_5$–$^1/_4$ oz) of food each day on average.

An individual may appear to eat far more, however, simply because it will carry food back to its nest, storing some rather than consuming it.

Hamster mixes

The typical ingredients of hamster mixes include the following: corn, dried peas, flaked maize and alfalfa. Most mixes also include peanuts and sunflower seed, which contain significantly higher amounts of oil (fat) and therefore should be fed only in restricted amounts to prevent a hamster becoming obese.

One of the main problems of feeding your hamster a seed mix is that it will inevitably pick out those seeds that it prefers, ignoring those that are less appealing, and this can distort its nutritional intake. Oats should always be avoided as a food for hamsters, because the sharp, pointed ends of the seeds mean they can become stuck in the animal's pouches, causing a painful impaction here, although groats, which are the dehulled form, are quite safe.

Dwarf Hamsters should also be offered smaller seeds than those

Right: *A hamster food mix may contain over a dozen ingredients.*

**CHAPTER
SIX**

▌ **Right:** *Food sticks are often preferred
▌ by hamsters to a standard food mix,*
but only feed these in moderation.

contained in a standard hamster mix
intended primarily for Syrian Hamsters.
Budgerigar seed mixes can be added
to their regular food or, alternatively,
millet sprays, which are the complete
grass seedheads, can be provided,
either whole or cut into short lengths.

Fresh foods

While dry food provides the basis of a
hamster's diet, other items will be valuable, with greenstuff being
a valuable source of vitamins as well as fibre. There are other
benefits associated with offering fresh foods, particularly during
the breeding period. It has been shown that hamsters kept
exclusively on dry food are likely to have smaller litters than
those given a more varied diet, including fresh items.

Grow your own

Even if you do not have access to a garden, you can still
guarantee a regular supply of fresh dandelion leaves for your
hamster throughout the year by following these simple steps:

1 Dig up the long root of a dandelion plant.
2 Cut it into sections with a sharp knife or pair of secateurs.
3 Plant these in a pot with the root just at the level of the
surface.
4 Keep moist and relatively warm on a well-lit windowsill to
encourage development of leaves.
5 Pick the leaves in rotation. Avoid overcropping any one plant.

Only offer greenstuff in small quantities, preferably on a regular basis, to prevent any disturbance to your hamster's digestive system. You can use a wide variety of vegetables or, alternatively, wild plants, such as dandelion, which is a valuable source of calcium, provided that these have been collected away from areas where chemical sprays may have been used, such as roadside verges, or where soiling by dogs is likely.

Your hamster will also eat carrot, which should be washed and peeled before being cut into smaller pieces, or even grated. Sweet dessert apple can be another beneficial addition to a hamster's diet, since it has been shown to reduce the incidence of cannibalism among breeding females with young. As with all fresh foods, however, remove any that is uneaten before it deteriorates. You will need to look inside the hamster's house as well as in the cage to spot any uneaten fresh foods which may have been stored there. In the wild, it appears that hamsters will

Below: *Fresh foods, such as dandelion, grated carrot, apple and cucumber, can all be offered as part of the regular diet.*

Left: *A hamster will strip a food stick down to the central wooden core. Indeed, some hamsters will even gnaw on the wood itself.*

generally only take dry foods back to their burrows. Although you can simply leave fresh foods on the hamster's bedding, it is much better to offer them in a food pot on their own. Do not add them to a dry seed mix because, being damp, they could cause the food to turn mouldy.

Additional protein

Dwarf Russians will frequently eat invertebrates as part of their regular diet, and so you can offer a few mealworms to these hamsters on a daily basis. These can be obtained from specialist bird or reptile food outlets, being the larval stage of the life-cycle of the Meal Beetle (*Tenebrio molitor*). These insects can be stored in a plastic container partly filled with chicken meal as a source of nutrition. Bran is another possibility as a foodstuff but it is less nutritious, which may, in turn, affect the feeding value of the mealworms.

If kept in a cool location to delay their development, mealworms may stay as larvae for several weeks. Being slow-moving, they are quite straightforward for the hamsters to catch, especially if offered in a food bowl.

Hard-boiled egg is also sometimes eaten by hamsters in small amounts, especially by females about to give birth or those nursing litters. Occasional flakes of grated Cheddar cheese are

Opposite: *Hamsters rely on their sharp incisor teeth to nibble off pieces of food which they can then stuff into their pouches. They seem to know almost instinctively just how large the pieces are that they can swallow.*

CHAPTER
SIX

another possibility, helping to boost the nutritional value of a seed-based diet, not just in terms of the level of protein but also with regard to its calcium content. Powdered baby milk may also be offered, especially to pregnant or suckling female hamsters. It can be given easily like a powdered supplement since it sticks well to the surface of cut apples.

Supplements and pelleted foods
An increasing range of vitamin and mineral supplements is available today, compensating for possible deficiencies in the hamster's diet. Some general pet supplements have been popular among small animal breeders for many years, whereas other products specifically intended for this group of pets are now becoming more widely available.

Supplements can be divided into liquid and powdered types, based on the way in which they are given. Those administered through drinking water are usually less comprehensive in terms of their ingredients than powdered products of this type. In all cases, it is very important to follow the recommendations for the use of these products carefully, since, especially over a period of time, overdosing is likely to be harmful.

However, if you are using a specially-formulated pelleted diet for your hamster rather than seeds, then supplementation is not usually recommended. At best, it represents a waste of money, while, at worst, it could even affect your pet's health adversely. This is because pelleted foods contain all the necessary ingredients, including vitamins and minerals, to meet a hamster's nutritional needs.

Left: *Hamster treats can be very useful for taming your pet to feed from your hand; they are larger than its ordinary food.*

Right: *Hamster treats are available in a wide range of sizes, but they must always be positioned so that they will not become soiled.*

Do not exceed the stated use-by date for any supplement; the same applies in the case of pellets. Otherwise, there is a risk that your hamster may not receive maximum benefit from them. Try to buy pellets from a busy pet store with a regular turnover in stock so that they should have a long use-by date. Storage conditions are also important, so keep the pellets in the dark in an airtight container. Concentrated liquid supplements in particular should be stored out of the light, which is why they are usually supplied in dark-coloured bottles.

Chews

It is is vital that hamsters have adequate opportunity to exercise their incisor teeth to prevent them from becoming overgrown and distorted. You can supply your pet with small branches or even twigs cut from non-poisonous trees. Apple branches can be useful for this purpose, but, as with all fruit trees, you must ensure that they have not been sprayed with any chemicals

Right: *In addition to edible treats, it is also possible to obtain wooden chews to keep your hamster's incisor teeth in shape.*

CHAPTER
SIX

recently, as hamsters may also eat the bark as they nibble it off.

Chews of various types manufactured from safe woods are also offered by many pet stores for hamsters. These can just be left on the floor of the hamster's quarters, although it is important to replace them if they become soiled. You may also

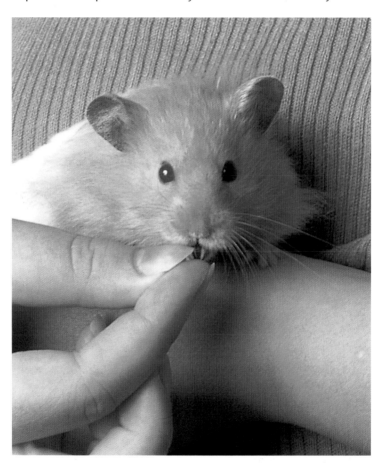

Above: *Once a hamster is used to taking food from you, it will do so regularly, but you should always be careful to let go, so that your pet does not inadvertently bite you.*

Edible chews

Another possible alternative is to offer edible chews, made from wholemeal bread. These can be prepared very easily, in a similar way to breadcrumbs, but children must be supervised when preparing chews of this type to ensure that they do not cut or burn themselves.

1 Cut the crusts off some wholemeal bread.
2 Bake them in the oven on a low heat until they are dry.
3 Allow to cool before offering them to your hamster.
4 Replace any uneaten crusts after a couple of days.
5 Take them out earlier if they become wet, as they will then turn mouldy.

want to offer your hamster a piece of cuttlebone, as sold for budgerigars. This will not only help to keep its teeth in shape but will also supplement the level of calcium and other important minerals in the animal's diet.

▌ Establishing a care routine

Hamsters do not require a great amount of daily care compared with many other pets, but they do need some daily attention and it is therefore advisable to establish a care routine. It is not a good idea to offer treats rather than their normal food on a very frequent basis, in spite of the fact that these may look more appealing. However, they can be given occasionally to your hamster.

Each day
- Change the water.
- Provide more food.
- Remove any fresh food which has not been eaten.
- Check the sleeping quarters for uneaten fresh food.

CHAPTER
SIX

┃ **Above:** *You can soon tame a young hamster to come and take food from you regularly when it wakes up.*

Cleanliness

A typical hamster cage is easier to clean than a tubular system. You simply need a large plastic bag or rubbish sack which will fit round the base so that you can tip in the contents of the cage. There should not be any wet areas, so that the bedding should slide in without difficulty, after which you can wipe the base over with clean paper towelling. Change the bedding in the hamster's house at the same time.

About once a month, wash the cage more thoroughly. This can be achieved easily using a dish-washing brush kept specifically for this purpose. Wash the cage off outside rather than down a sink, using either a detergent or a special disinfectant added to the water. Next rinse the cage off thoroughly and shake it dry before wiping it over with paper towelling. The same applies to a tubular housing system. These usually have to be dismantled, at least partially, in order to be cleaned – even to have stale food removed.

The advantage of a ball toy

You will need to clean out the quarters thoroughly once or twice a week, and it helps if you have a carrier or a ball-type toy where your hamster can be confined safely while you are carrying out this task. This is a large acrylic container, which splits into two halves. The hamster can be placed inside and moves the ball along by using its feet. Hamsters generally enjoy being in a ball toy for short periods, but it is definitely not recommended to leave them confined here for more than about 15 minutes, because they will become tired. Children must also be closely supervised with a hamster in a ball, because they may be tempted to roll the ball along themselves, which will be very disorientating for the pet within. Nor should it ever be placed in direct sunlight, because the interior will soon become very hot.

| Handling and taming your hamster

Young hamsters can become very tame if handled every day, but you may need to start slowly to win your new pet's confidence. Never suddenly attempt to pick up your hamster as this is likely to result in you being bitten. You must let your hamster become familiar with the scent of your hand in the first instance. It will soon realise that you present no threat to it, but if it is grabbed suddenly, a hamster will react and try to defend itself by using its teeth, particularly when held tightly around the body. This reflects the fact its eyesight is relatively poor, and so it may not focus on your hand. Scent is a much more important sense than sight for hamsters in this situation.

You should always try to coax the hamster on to the palm of your hand rather than picking it up quickly. Once the hamster is sitting on your hand, you can lift it safely, cupping your hands together if necessary. It is obviously important not to let your pet

Above: *Always keep a watchful eye on a hamster when it is out of its quarters, because these rodents can rapidly scamper off and disappear into a room.*

fall at any stage, because this could result in a limb fracture or even a fatal injury. Be sure that any dogs or cats are out of the room when you take your hamster out of its quarters.

Even when the hamster is in its quarters, you can still continue the taming process by encouraging it to take titbits

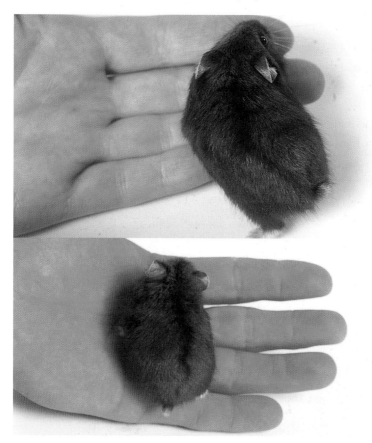

Above: *Scent is very important in a hamster's life, because the eyesight of these rodents is relatively poor. Always allow your hamster to sniff your hand; it will soon realise that it has nothing to fear and then you can encourage it to step on to your hand.*

from your hand. Keep these handling sessions relatively short,
particularly at first, and try to avoid disturbing a sleeping hamster
for this purpose, because it may react instinctively by biting,
being suddenly aroused from its slumber.

Right and below:
*Picking up a hamster is
quite straightforward, but
never try to grasp your pet
tightly in your hand at
any stage, because this is
likely to cause it to react
by biting you.*

▌Escapes

Hamsters can move surprisingly fast on occasions so if your
hamster does try to scurry off, place your hand down in front of
your pet to bring it to a relative standstill before scooping it up.
Should the hamster actually disappear, the first thing to do will
be to close the door of the room, in the hope that it will not
have managed to scamper further afield in the home. A loose
hamster will often seek to hide at first under a chair or behind
a piece of furniture, so start by looking around these areas. Take
very great care if moving any furniture, because there could be
a risk of inadvertently injuring your pet badly in the process.
Also, be sure to keep other pets out of the room until your
hamster has been caught.

Should all else fail, then you will need to abandon your search
until after dark. This is the time that a hamster is most likely to
make itself known, particularly when the house is quiet, as you
may hear it scratching or scampering around the room.

It is especially important to ensure that you recapture your pet
as soon as possible, because if it manages to slip down beneath
the floorboards not only will it be difficult to retrieve here, but
there is a real risk of damage to electrical cabling if the hamster
decides to use its teeth in this part of the home. You may be able
to use a safe rodent trap, more normally used for rats and mice,
to catch your hamster without difficulty but, alternatively, a stack
of books and a bucket can be used in an emergency.

Stack the books to the top of the bucket so the hamster can
climb up, easily lured by the presence of food at the end of a thin
piece of wood extending over the bucket, which is lined with soft
hamster bedding. Rubbing a piece of apple up the books should
encourage it to clamber up the pile. Hopefully, your hamster will
then try to reach the food but topples over into the bucket, where
it can be safely retrieved unhurt the following morning.

CHAPTER
SIX

▌ Showing your hamster

Try to visit some shows before entering your own hamsters, so you can see what is involved. Generally, hamsters are exhibited in special uniform cages known as show pens. This helps the judge in arriving at a decision, because the cages themselves will not be a distraction in any way. The show pens are also designed so that the hamsters can be taken out easily for judging purposes.

Entering a show

By joining one or more of the hamster clubs in your area, you will learn when shows are taking place through their newsletters, although the larger events are often advertised in specialist magazines as well. Entering a show is easy. Be sure to send for the show schedule and an entry form as early as possible before the event, enclosing a self-addressed, stamped envelope whenever writing to the show secretary.

You will obviously need to decide on which of your hamsters to enter – it is important to avoid showing any that are in less than top condition. Not only will they not have a realistic prospect of winning the class but also, being slightly out of condition, they could be more vulnerable to picking up an infection as the result of the change in their surroundings.

The schedule must be read closely because it lists all the classes, and you will need to fill in the entry form carefully on this basis. If you are in doubt, ask for advice because your hamsters will be disqualified on the day if they have been entered incorrectly for any reason. You must send the completed entry form back with the appropriate entry fees well before the closing date.

It is then a matter of ensuring as far as possible that your hamsters will be looking at their best on the day of the event. Long-coated hamsters will need to be groomed carefully, while any staining on the fur, which will be most apparent in the case

Right: *Although Syrian Hamsters are most commonly seen at shows, other types of hamster are being exhibited as well, such as the Winter White Dwarf Russian.*

of pale-coloured varieties, will need to be washed off with a little baby shampoo, keeping this well away from the eyes. Be sure the coat has adequate time to dry before the event. In the case of short-coated hamsters, especially satins, wiping the coat with a piece of silk material on a daily basis for a week or so prior to a show can help to improve the desirable glossy sheen. You also need to check well in advance that the show pens are in good condition, with none of the paintwork being chipped, carrying out any repairs or repainting as necessary.

Going to a show
It is better to take the hamsters to the show in carriers rather than show pens. This allows them to settle more readily in these surroundings as they can be supplied with bedding, which will serve as a temporary nest. You can then transfer your hamsters to their show pens at the venue. A thin layer of shavings will be needed as the floor covering, although for long-coated hamsters, cat litter should be used to prevent the bedding becoming caught up in the fur. Contact the officials on arrival, so that you can bench your hamsters, placing them on the staging, and then wait for the judge's verdict. No food and water should be provided until after judging has taken place.

Try to arrive well in advance, so as to give your hamsters an opportunity to settle down before being judged. This is carried out

CHAPTER
SIX

by transferring the hamster on to a judging frame or board, which consists of a piece of mesh with a wooden surround. Judges use this to take hamsters out of their show pen, having lowered the front, to give a clear view of the hamster's underparts, including the colour of the fur. After being used, the judging board is carefully disinfected to prevent any spread of infection.

The hamsters are not actually judged against each other but awarded points compared with the ideal standard for that particular variety, and it is the hamster awarded the most points that will win the class. It is important to have a clear indication in your mind of what the judges consider to be desirable – this can only really be obtained by attending shows and studying the winning entries. This will give you an insight into the features that are required, including the correct depth of coloration and patterning as appropriate. You can then aim to replicate these strengths in your own hamster stud.

Exclusions

Although moulting will preclude a hamster from taking part temporarily in a show, other flaws can represent a permanent exclusion. Torn or otherwise damaged ears, for example, fit into this category, as will any deviated claws. There is obviously no reason as to why such hamsters cannot play an important role in your breeding programme, however, as these features will not be transmitted to their offspring, being caused by injury. In contrast, hamsters displaying poor type (appearance), coloration or markings are not suitable for exhibition purposes, but they can still prove to be delightful pets.

What makes an exhibition hamster?

There are a number of features that help to set a top exhibition hamster apart from its pet counterparts, with some of these characteristics being less obvious than others. They include:

Type

Judging standards generally call for the head to be as broad between the eyes as it is long, while the front of the face, described as the muzzle, must have a short, blunt appearance rather than being elongated. The body itself needs to be broad but condition is important. Judges will not be fooled by an overweight individual, whose skin hangs down rather than remaining taut against the sides of the body when the hamster is on the ground or a judging board.

Size

Exhibition hamsters of either sex tend to be relatively large in size, compared with those bred as pets, but judges do make allowances for the fact that females are naturally bigger than males. The eyes should be quite prominent on the face, with the ears also being relatively large, undamaged and kept in an upright, alert pose.

Coloration, markings and coat type

These must all conform as closely as possible to the desired characteristics of the variety concerned. Often with new varieties, while their coloration is good, their type is lacking and it takes careful breeding over a number of generations to combine both features successfully.

Condition

This can make the difference between winning and losing, especially in the face of fierce competition. Clean fur, with a good shine to the coat, is essential, with the fur itself having to be dense over the belly area as well as the body.

CHAPTER SEVEN

Breeding

*Although hamsters do breed freely under suitable conditions,
this is likely to be a relatively expensive undertaking, as a
result of their housing requirements. Yet it can also be very
rewarding, if you have the necessary facilities available.
Here are some basic guidelines to help you.*

Breeding hamsters is not to be undertaken lightly because,
like many rodents, they have large litters, and the anti-
social nature of Syrian Hamsters in particular means that
they must be housed separately soon after weaning. You therefore
need to be absolutely sure that you can either find good homes
for the offspring or are prepared to keep them before pairing up
your hamsters in readiness for breeding.

▌ Avoiding breeding conflicts

Hamster pairings need to be carried out carefully to minimize
the likelihood of the smaller male in particular being injured,
especially with Syrians. You must never be tempted to place
the male directly in the female's accommodation, as this is likely
to end up with him being attacked. It is much safer to introduce
them on neutral ground. Many breeders use a so-called
'honeymoon cage' for this purpose. There are special acrylic
containers with plastic hoods and a removable central partition,
which are suitable for this purpose, although you can simply place
an acrylic divider in a converted aquarium set-up for hamsters.

Above: *A pregnant Chinese hamster. Their gestation period is about 21 days, whereas that of the Dwarf Russian is usually around 18 days.*

Start by placing one of the hamsters in the enclosure, allowing it to explore and leave its scent here, before transferring it back to its usual accommodation. Then place the other member of the prospective pair in the container so that its scent can merge with that of the other hamster. At this stage, you should introduce the partition into the enclosure, then place one of the hamsters on each side of it.

Once the hamsters are settled and start to show an interest in each other, remove the partition in the early evening, because this is when a female is most likely to accept a mate. Watch the pair carefully and, hopefully, there will be no signs of serious aggression. It will soon be apparent if the female is ready to accept the male, as she will stand with her tail in a vertical position, with mating occurring soon afterwards. The pair should be left together for 30 minutes or so, with mating likely to occur repeatedly during this time.

Afterwards, the hamsters should be separated and transferred to separate quarters. Pregnant females should ideally be kept in a converted aquarium to prevent any risk of their young becoming stuck in the bars of the cage once they leave the nest.

Pregnancy

Should the first attempt have failed, as the result of evident disagreement, then separate the hamsters immediately. Reintroduce them, using the same method, after a couple of days, since females come into oestrus roughly every four days. It will be a good sign if there is a whitish, sticky discharge around the female's reproductive opening after the pair have been together. Some breeders like to try a second mating four days later, but should this occur, it gives no guarantee that the female is not already pregnant, although if she is aggressive towards her mate on this occasion it is a likely indicator.

Pregnancy in the case of the Syrian is among the shortest of all mammals, lasting just 16 days. It is very important not to handle or disturb the pregnant female more than necessary, particularly as the time for the birth of the young, known as pups, approaches.

You will start to notice obvious signs of pregnancy in the female about 10 days after the mating, in terms of an obvious increase in the body size.

Right: One of the most obvious signs of pregnancy in hamsters, as in the case of this Dwarf Russian, is that females are soon likely to appear much plumper.

CHAPTER
SEVEN

Birth and rearing

The female is likely to give birth in her nest, and it is particularly important that you restrain your curiosity and do not dive in to look at the pups. The presence of your scent in amongst her young may cause the female to cannibalize her offspring. If you do suspect that something could be wrong, then take a pencil and rub the blunt end in the nest litter of the cage, perhaps even brushing the female hamster's fur gently with it to mask any strange scent. You can then use this to prize the nest apart gently, enabling you to see the pups.

Hamsters are totally helpless at birth, lacking any fur and with their eyes closed. They are very small, and it has been recorded

Above: *This litter of Roborovski's Dwarf Hamsters are just six days old and developing rapidly. Keep disturbances to a minimum while the young are still in the nest.*

Right: *A Roborovski's Dwarf Hamster at six weeks of age, just after being weaned. They need to stay with their mother slightly longer than other pet hamsters.*

that females will sometimes defend their litters by carrying their tiny young in their cheek pouches to another nest.

The pups develop very rapidly, however, with their fur emerging by the time they are about five days old. Subsequently, they may start eating solid food brought back to the nest by the female from a week onwards, with their eyes opening around this time.

No special foods are needed during the rearing period, but it is very important that the female has sufficient drinking water because her fluid consumption will rise dramatically during this period while she is producing milk for her offspring. Any shortage is likely to result in the young dying from a lack of milk, or she may cannibalize them.

Bread and milk and hard-boiled egg are sometimes offered as rearing foods, but take particular care to ensure that these do not become sour, since they will be exceedingly harmful to the hamsters in this state. You also need to wash the food bowl out thoroughly, using a detergent. Make sure you rinse the bowl afterwards.

Weaning

The young will need to be weaned at between three and four weeks of age, because after this age, especially in the case of Syrians, they are likely to be attacked by the female. They can be housed in a group together for a further two or three weeks before they, too, will need to be separated. Young hamsters can attain maturity at just six weeks old, although planned breeding is

CHAPTER
SEVEN

unlikely to start until a female is at least four months of age.

It is best to wait for a couple of months before allowing the female to have another litter, although she may start to cycle again within a few days of her young being removed. Avoid overbreeding, even if you are lucky enough to have a really good female, because this is likely to be reflected in the quality of the young. Most breeders aim for two or three litters during a female's lifetime, although, in theory, she could produce at least three times as many in this period.

Below: *The markings of related hamsters are likely to be variable, as shown by this Black Mottled Dwarf Russian and her youngster.*

Dwarf Russian and Chinese Hamsters

If these hamsters are being kept in groups, it is quite usual for only the dominant female to breed and, in the case of the Chinese Hamster, she is very likely to become aggressive towards her intended partner during her period of pregnancy. There is obviously a risk in leaving them together, but, assuming the male remains, the female usually becomes more tolerant again after giving birth.

Less aggression is usually observed in the case of Dwarf Russian Hamsters, and both members of the pair frequently care for the young. Extra dietary protein is important for these smaller

Above: *Young Chinese Hamsters. They will start to leave their nest for periods from the age of two weeks onwards.*

hamsters, particularly Roborovski's, during the breeding period, to ensure successful mating and rearing of the young.

Colour breeding

The genetics of colour breeding in hamsters is a complex subject, but there are certain pitfalls of which you need to be aware to avoid the likely occurrence of problems in pups. For example, satin-coated hamsters, irrespective of their colour, should not be paired together because this will result in a noticeable thinning of the coat. It is also thought that male white Chinese Hamsters are infertile.

The other major genetic problem that needs to be borne in mind is linked with certain varieties that carry the anophthalamic 'Wh' gene in their make-up. These are Dark-eared Whites,

CHAPTER
SEVEN

Above: *A litter of young Syrian Hamsters which are just over three weeks old, with their Cinnamon mother. Not all pairings are recommended.*

Dominant Spots, Roans and all White-bellied Hamsters and, as a result, they should not be paired together but outcrossed to other colours. The harmful recessive gene will otherwise result in some of the hamsters being born either without eyes (anophthalmia) or, alternatively, with very small eyes which is a condition described as microphthalmia.

Pairings

All the characteristics of the hamster, including its coloration and coat length, are determined by its genes. These are carried on paired structures called chromosomes, which are present in the nucleus of every living cell in its body. When conception occurs, a hamster receives half its genes from its mother and half from its father.

The way in which these combine is entirely random, and this

is why there are often hamsters of different colours and coat types in a litter. In a hamster's genetic make-up, the genes on the opposing chromosomes may be the same or they may differ.

Under these circumstances, one colour will be dominant over the other, with the result that the hamster can then carry the other colour in its genetic make-up, although this will not be apparent from its appearance. The normal colour of the Syrian is dominant over the Albino, for example, so that if these two colours are mated together all the offspring are golden in colour.

Each of these will then carry a hidden albino gene, however, so that if they were to mate together, out of every four pups, three will be golden and one will be albino in colour on average, because of the way in which the genes from the parents are likely to combine together. This is why accurate pedigree records are vital in helping you predict the different colours that are likely to be produced from a particular pairing.

Breeding failures

There can be a number of reasons for breeding failure. These include the following:

Obesity: Check the weights of the hamsters by placing each one in a container on scales. You may need to slim your hamsters down, increasing the quantity of greenstuff being offered.

The time of year: Hamsters are most likely to breed successfully during the spring and summer months rather than during the winter in temperate areas. Males are likely to be infertile during the depths of winter, while females do not come into oestrus. This is a reflection of both decreased day length and the lower temperature.

Age: A young female may not mate willingly with a young male. It is better to use a mature male in this situation.

CHAPTER EIGHT

Hamster
health

Although hamsters generally have quite short lifespans, they are not especially prone to illness, especially if fed correctly and kept in clean surroundings. You will soon become used to your hamster's normal behaviour, and this should then help you to identify possible health problems in future.

amsters are generally very healthy animals and rarely need veterinary treatment, but if you are concerned about your pet's health, you should seek advice from an experienced small animal vet without delay. A hamster's condition can deteriorate rapidly, and thus prompt action can dramatically increase the likelihood of treatment being successful.

CHAPTER
EIGHT

BASIC VETERINARY CARE

Hamsters are most likely to fall ill in the period from weaning onwards until they have become established in their new home. Always spend a few moments each day just checking for any indication of possible illness in your pet. Signs of concern can be when a hamster is eating less than usual or drinking more. Also, it may not be as active as normal or its droppings could change in consistency.

■ Tail
Watch for staining under the tail, which can indicate diarrhoea, while the tail itself is vulnerable to being injured in a fight.

■ Coat
There should be no thinning of the coat, which could indicate a health problem such as ringworm, or may be seen in old age. It should not be matted either, or tangled as can occur in long-haired hamsters which have not been groomed regularly.

■ Paws
A hamster uses its paws both for climbing and holding its food. Its claws are normally quite sharp and can occasionally become too long, which will cause your hamster to have difficulty in climbing. They should be trimmed back carefully, because of the blood supply running down the claw.

■ **Skin**

Most of the hamster's body is covered with hair, so that the condition of the skin is not very obvious over most of the body, aside from areas where it is exposed, although any build-up of scurf in the coat is indicative of an underlying skin problem. Skin problems may often have a nutritional link.

■ **Ears**

A hamster's ears rarely need attention, but sometimes, the ear flaps themselves end up being torn or injured usually as the result of a fight. The area will heal without problems, but the hamster is likely to be permanently disfigured as a consequence.

■ **Eyes**

The eyes should be bright and alert with no sign of discharge or cloudiness.

■ **Nose**

There should be no sign of mucus around the nostrils.

■ **Cheek pouches**

On occasions, the cheek pouches can become impacted with food, causing a permanent swelling at the side of the hamster's face.

■ **Mouth and teeth**

The sharp incisor teeth at the front of the mouth are vital to allow the hamster to gnaw its food effectively. They continue growing throughout its life, so that if one is deviated, this will affect the hamster's ability to eat.

CHAPTER
EIGHT

DIGESTIVE PROBLEMS

You are most likely to encounter health worries with newly-acquired hamsters, and these can often be linked with the change in their environment and possibly diet as well.

Wet tail

The most serious of these illnesses is the digestive illness often known as 'wet tail' because of the diarrhoea which causes staining of the fur around this part of the body. This condition is relatively common in Long-haired Syrians but is rarely encountered in the Dwarf Russian or Chinese Hamsters.

■ **Symptoms:** An affected individual is clearly ill, being hunched up with its fur raised. It will lose interest in its food.

Treatment: Treating wet tail, or proliferative ileitis as it also known because it causes inflammation of the part of the small intestine known as the ileum, is difficult but can sometimes be successful. Fluid therapy is very important to prevent the hamster suffering from fatal dehydration as a result of the diarrhoea. Antibiotics can help, but it is essential that these are used only under veterinary supervision because some types are deadly to hamsters.

Tyzzer's Disease

This is another serious digestive problem which can strike young hamsters. It is caused by a bacterium known as *Bacillus piliformis*. Similar treatment in this case is also needed, with fluid therapy and the antibiotic oxytetracycline offering the best hope of a

Above: *A healthy hamster, even a long-haired one, has a sleek appearance. When suffering from a digestive disorder, hamsters usually appear hunched up, drink more and prove less active.*

recovery. It is also very important to disinfect the hamster's quarters thoroughly, since this particular infection can survive for up to a year.

Other problems

In some cases, diarrhoea is not necessarily caused directly by an infective organism. It can be the result of a hamster gorging itself on fresh food, but there is still an underlying danger, which can be linked with any form of severe gut disturbance. The abnormal movement of the intestinal tract can cause it to become compressed, leading to what is described as an intussusception. This can also result from a blockage in the intestines if, for example, the hamster has eaten unsuitable bedding. Bloody diarrhoea is seen in such cases, with the rear part of the digestive tract sometimes protruding from the body. In this case, the only hope is surgery but, sadly, this is usually not successful.

CHAPTER
EIGHT

Constipation

This digestive problem is most likely to be encountered in young hamsters, as well as old individuals, and the most obvious sign will be that your pet is not producing any droppings. The cause in young hamsters is often that they have not successfully located the drinking bottle. If you suspect constipation, you should always give the young hamster an opportunity to drink to see whether it is very thirsty.

In the case of old hamsters, there may be a loss of tone of their digestive tract, so increasing the amount of greenstuff in their diet may help to prevent a recurrence. This is probably the best way of dealing with the problem, although very small amounts of a laxative, such as a few drops of olive oil, may help at the outset. It can be given through a clean eye-dropper, which will prevent oil matting the fur. You do need to be very careful not to cause diarrhoea, however, by overdosing your pet with a laxative under these circumstances.

Right: *Constipation is more likely to arise in obese individuals which have a poor diet comprised mainly of sunflower seeds.*

PARASITES

Hamsters can be susceptible to both external parasites, found on the skin, and internal parasites, which can occur within their bodies. However, if you have a single hamster at home, it is unlikely to acquire parasites.

Fleas

Bear in mind that if you also have a cat or dog, and especially if your hamster is allowed to scamper over the floor on occasions, then it could acquire fleas from them. Check with your vet for advice on what will be a safe treatment if your hamster does suffer from fleas, which are likely to cause it to scratch repeatedly.

Above: *Excessive grooming can indicate skin irritation caused by parasites.*

Mites

These can only be seen under the microscope, but they too can cause itching of the skin as well as hair loss. Their presence and identity can be confirmed by means of skin scrapings of the affected area, which are then examined under a microscope. Treatment often consists of drops given orally, but bear in mind that these parasites can be spread on grooming equipment so this should be replaced, as a precautionary measure, to prevent possible reinfection. The cage, too, should be thoroughly cleaned.

Internal parasites

These can sometimes be present in a hamster's digestive tract without causing obvious signs of illness. There is a very slight risk with the

CHAPTER
EIGHT

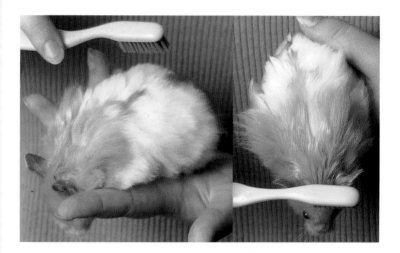

Above: *Long-haired hamsters will benefit from being groomed with a soft toothbrush. This provides a good opportunity to check the animal's coat, but always brush away from the head to avoid the hamster's prominent eyes.*

dwarf tapeworm (*Hymenolepis nana*), however, because this might potentially be transmitted to people. As a precautionary measure, children should be taught from the outset always to wash their hands thoroughly after handling a hamster or attending to its needs.

Ringworm

In spite of its name, ringworm is not a parasitic illness but is caused by a fungus. This, too, can cause localized hair loss, particularly in circular patches, and may be linked with infection in dogs and cats, particularly if they have access to the hamster's bedding. The fungal spores are also spread easily on grooming equipment. It is another zoonosis – a disease that can be spread to people – causing reddish, circular patches in the skin in this case, but it is very rarely seen in hamsters.

ORAL PROBLEMS

If your hamster appears to be having difficulty in eating and is losing weight, then its teeth should be checked in case they have started to grow at an abnormal angle. Careful trimming of the teeth by your vet should resolve the problem.

Beware of offering your hamster too many treats, because these may be linked with dental decay and even abscesses. Eating becomes painful, and there may be excessive amounts of saliva trailing out of the mouth, along with obvious swelling of the affected area. It may be necessary to extract a tooth under these circumstances, although this is quite a drastic step.

Similar signs may result if an object becomes stuck in the mouth, and also if there is a problem affecting the cheek pouches, so veterinary advice will be essential to determine the cause of the problem and advise on the most appropriate treatment. In a few cases, the cheek pouches become everted, and this, too, will need to be corrected so that they can continue functioning properly.

Left: *Although you can check a hamster's incisor teeth quite easily, see a vet if you suspect a problem here.*

PROBLEMS OF OLD AGE

Aside from constipation, thinning of the coat is a common sign of old age in hamsters. This may be linked with hormonal problems, especially if the hair loss is present in corresponding patches on both sides of the body.

Diabetes

Both Dwarf Russian and Chinese Hamsters can also be vulnerable to sugar diabetes (*diabetes mellitus*), another hormonal disorder, as they grow older.

Symptoms
■   Affected individuals are abnormally thirsty, drinking large volumes of water.
■   They produce correspondingly copious volumes of urine.
■   Their eyes often become cloudy, revealing the presence of cataracts linked with this condition.

Hamsters can live for some time with diabetes, but stock from affected bloodlines should not be bred from, because of the likelihood that this is an inherited weakness.

Kidney problems

These can also result in an increased thirst and urinary output, and are likely to become more common in old age with the effects being irreversible.

Tumours

These are not generally common in hamsters, but males may develop testicular tumours as they become older, which cause a distortion of this part of the body. Surgery to remove the testes should resolve the problem. Other tumours affecting the scent glands on the sides of the body are not unknown either.

Above: *A number of health problems in hamsters are caused by ageing.*

Heart problems

Hamsters can sometimes suffer from heart problems in old age, and these can lead to breathing difficulty. Your pet will also have a lack of energy. The best thing to do will be to slow down its lifestyle by preventing it from exercising on a wheel, and deterring it from climbing around its quarters by transferring it to an acrylic or glass tank. Cut back also on fatty seeds, such as sunflower, in its diet.

Lymphocytic Chorio-meningitis Virus (LCMV)

This infection is found mainly in wild mice but, on rare occasions, it can be spread to hamsters if they are allowed to come into contact with these rodents, and may in turn be transmitted to people. Tilting of the head has been recorded as a sign of this infection in hamsters, whereas in people LCMV infection is most likely to cause symptoms resembling those of severe influenza.

CHAPTER
EIGHT

EMERGENCY CARE

The home environment can sometimes hold dangers for hamsters, and their small size means that they can be vulnerable to the effects of shock, so handling should be kept to a minimum. In most cases of this type, your pet will need veterinary care. As always, remember to wash your hands thoroughly after handling your hamster or attending to its needs.

Attacks on hamsters

The most common emergency situation involving a hamster is often the need to rescue it from being killed by a cat or, less often, a dog. If you manage to save the hamster and it is still alive, try not to handle it more than strictly necessary, because it will be in a state of severe shock. It will be much better simply to leave your pet in a dark and reasonably warm location where it can hopefully recover over the course of a couple of hours, provided that it is showing no signs of major injury.

A veterinary check-up at an early stage is to be recommended, however, if the cat's teeth caused any injury to the hamster. This is because cats have highly unpleasant bacteria in their mouths, which can be transferred under the skin as the result of a bite. Here they can develop, leading to a generalized infection which could cause the subsequent death of the hamster. Your vet may therefore prescribe a course of antibiotics as a precautionary measure for your hamster.

In cases where hamsters have attacked each other, abscesses can also form at the site of injuries and these will need to be bathed to draw the pus out of the wound. If there is bleeding, pressing gently at the site of the injury for a few moments should trigger the clotting process.

FIRST AID

Housing problems

It is always important to watch your pet's behaviour closely in case it does develop unusual symptoms, which could be linked to its housing. Hamsters can sometimes injure themselves in their quarters, for example, by rubbing the insides of their legs bare when using a wheel with an open metal tread. The problem will be resolved simply by changing the wheel to a solid plastic track. If you find that your hamster has actually become caught up in its wheel or elsewhere in its quarters, then try to free it very gently, to avoid causing any further injury.

Allergic reactions

Problems may sometimes arise with bedding, too, as it is believed that some hamsters can develop an allergic reaction to shavings, resulting in hair loss on their underparts. The feet can sometimes become swollen, although there may be other allergens in the home that could be responsible.

In the case of a hamster that is kept in a bedroom, perfume and furniture polish are potential allergic hazards, while cigarette smoke can be another cause of this problem. Sneezing is common when the allergen is being inhaled although, in other respects, the hamster will appear quite healthy with its appetite unaffected.

When faced with a problem of this type, make some rapid changes in your pet's environment to see if its condition improves. You can also alter its bedding and use a different food, or simply remove dyed biscuit meal from the seed mix, in case the hamster is allergic to the colouring agent. Cutting back on oil-rich seeds, such as sunflower, in the hamster's diet is also recommended as a preliminary step when trying to isolate the cause of an allergic reaction.

CHAPTER
EIGHT

Poisoning

There are a number of foodstuffs that we enjoy, notably chocolate and salted peanuts, which can be deadly to hamsters, so never give your pet these foods. Chocolate can easily kill a hamster because it contains a chemical that depresses the respiratory system. In terms of vegetables, it is also a good idea to avoid avocado, as this could possibly be poisonous as well.

Fractures

If you suspect that your hamster may have fractured a limb as a result of a fall or on its playwheel, avoid handing it more than is strictly necessary as it will be in shock. You will need to seek veterinary advice. Often, it is very difficult to set the fracture as hamsters will gnaw off any supporting dressing, but usually the bones do heal and the hamster will be relatively unimpeded by its injury. It is necessary to keep it in a tank where it cannot climb or exercise on a wheel for about six weeks to ensure that the healing process can occur.

Heat stroke and hibernation

Hamsters are surprisingly ill-equipped to survive in hot surroundings when the temperature rises much above 20°C (68°F). They will start to develop signs of heat stroke, often referred to as 'Sleeper Disease'. The hamster adopts a rigid position and will die rapidly unless it is moved without delay to a much cooler location. Unfortunately, if there has been long-standing heat exposure, resulting in dehydration, then associated kidney failure may prove fatal, so encourage an affected hamster to drink freely during its recuperation phase.

At the other extreme, if the environmental temperature drops down much below 5°C (41°F), then hamsters become torpid. This is potentially less serious, although because of the slowing of the hamster's vital body processes, its breathing rate plummets, giving the impression that it is dead. When it is transferred to a warmer environment, however, the hamster should recover spontaneously.

Beware if you have a cold !

Finally, if you develop a cold, it is a good idea to ask someone else in the family to look after your hamster and not to handle your pet until you are feeling much better. This is because they can pick up our cold viruses as well as influenza. Unfortunately, these illnesses frequently cause pneumonia in hamsters, and there is no effective cure for them.

FIRST AID